SHAKESPEARE

FOR BEGINNERS™

WRITTEN BY BRANDON TOROPOV
ILLUSTRATED BY JOE LEE

For Beginners LLC
62 East Starrs Plain Road
Danbury, CT 06810 USA
www.forbeginnersbooks.com

A For Beginners® Documentary Comic Book
Originally published by Writers and Readers, Inc.
Copyright © 1997, 1999

Cataloging-in-Publication information is available from the Library of Congress

ISBN-10 # 1-934389-29-3 Trade
ISBN-13 # 978-1-934389-29-4 Trade

Manufactured in the United States of America

For Beginners® and Beginners Documentary Comic Books® are published by
For Beginners LLC

Reprint Edition

FROM BRANDON TOROPOV:

For Jim Clay, now working on a new show.

ACKNOWLEDGMENTS

My heartfelt thanks go out to Glenn Thompson, Ron David, Glenn KnicKrehm, Leslie Hamilton, Bob Tragert — and above all to my wife Mary, whose patience and encouragement knew no bounds.

ILLUSTRATION DEDICATION FROM JOE LEE:

To Mary Bess Bohon, a 'Dark Lady' who has brought such illumination to my life.

And to Ron David, as well, for providing me with such opportunities to expand my creativity and for accepting them when I do.

The Plays

The Poems

Welcome To Shakespeare

For more than 350 years, William Shakespeare has been the world's most popular playwright. On stage, in movies, and on television, his plays are watched by eager audiences all over the world. People read his plays again and again for the sheer pleasure.

Unfortunately, many of us are intimidated by Shakespeare.

That is where **Shakespeare for Beginners** comes in. Even if you've had trouble with Shakespeare in the past, **Shakespeare for Beginners** will make him accessible—and fun. This book will help you enjoy and appreciate Shakespeare quickly, without feeling like you're doing 'homework' to prepare for him.

How will we do that?

$\mathring{\text{S}}$imple, really: For the most part, we will let the stories tell themselves. Shakespeare was capable —is capable— of stopping people in their tracks and persuading them to listen to a story. The writing Shakespeare is best known for is work for the theater, and theater is, first and foremost, *direct*.

It has to grab the audience and make it pay attention . . . <u>RIGHT</u> <u>NOW.</u>

Newcomers to Shakespeare are often surprised to find that his plays are filled with action, his characters are believable, and the situations they find themselves in are exactly like our own—greed, power, ambition, love, jealousy, old age, racism.

People haven't changed much in the last four centuries. It is both comforting and terrifying to see aspects of your own personality magnified by Shakespeare's genius in the 'overthinking' Prince of Denmark, the jealous Moor of Venice, the noble Cordelia, or the bitchy Kate. And the language, once you relax in its presence, is downright thrilling.

Five Things You Should Know About Shakespeare's Theatrical World

1: Prose and poetry were both used by dramatists in Shakespeare's day. **Rhyming couplets** (two lines that rhyme) often alerted the audience to the end of a scene, or to a new situation or locale in a scene to come. (Rhyme could also occur within the scenes, of course.)

2: The women's parts were played by men. **Ingenues** (young girls) were usually played by boys.

3: There were no **'blackouts'**—no time when the **'lights'** (actually, *candles*) went out. So any time a character died in front of the audience, the body had to be carried off the stage.

4: The departure of all characters from the stage signaled the end of a scene; and, according to the convention of the time, a character could not take part in both the ending of one scene and the beginning of the next one.

5: The audiences represented a broad cross-section of English society, so successful writers like Shakespeare had to write on at least two levels; they had to appeal to the best —and least— educated people in the audience; they had to know how to use both rude'n'crude humor and refined classical *allusions*. So the plays themselves have a 'built in' aid to understanding.

❀ **Allusions** are sort of literary 'name-dropping'; you mention a name from Greek mythology or a phrase from a famous poem, and the truly refined reader 'gets' it.

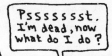

Pssssssst. I'm dead, now what do I do?

Before we go further, let's have a look at the man himself.

3

What do people really know about this guy?

Not much. He was baptized on April 26, 1564, in Stratford-on-Avon, England. His father John was a glover who was named to several important town posts, and may have had financial difficulties later in life. William wasted no time getting started in life. At the age of eighteen, he married Anne Hathaway. The couple had three children: Susanna (born in 1583), and the twins Hamnet and Judith (1585). (Hamnet died in 1596.) Nobody is certain exactly what Shakespeare did between 1583 and 1592. Somewhere along the line, he became an actor and began writing plays. In 1592, a jealous playwright named Robert Greene attacked Shakespeare in print, and made fun of the idea of an actor writing plays. Shakespeare apparently wasn't too impressed by Mr. Green's criticism; he continued to write and perform, and he became an important figure in the London literary and theatrical scene. He published two narrative poems, **Venus and Adonis** (1593) and **The Rape of Lucrece** (1594). A writer named Francis Meres took notice of Shakespeare in 1598, listing twelve of his plays and complimenting his privately circulated poetry. The well-connected acting company with which Shakespeare was associated, the Lord Chamberlain's Men, built a theater in 1598 called the Globe; he owned an interest in the playhouse.

In 1603, when James I became King, the Lord Chamberlain's Men became the King's Men. Over the years, some of Shakespeare's plays were published in unauthorized editions (but many of his plays were never published during his lifetime); a collection of his sonnets appeared in 1609. After the Globe burned down in 1613, Shakespeare seems to have stopped writing and performing. He spent the last years of his life at Stratford, in a home he'd bought in 1597 called New Place. He died in 1616 and was buried in Stratford. Shakespeare's life was so unspectacular that some people have found it hard to believe that such an 'ordinary' man with so little formal schooling could create the greatest body of work in the English language. (As if genius could be taught in school!) Most scholars now accept the fact that Shakespeare did indeed write his own plays.

Those are pretty slim pickings for the biography of a genius. Fortunately, it is Shakespeare's writing, not his personal life, that has captivated audiences for nearly four centuries. That writing is the Shakespeare we'll be looking at in the following pages.

In most cases textual excerpts and act and scene divisions reflect Nicolaus Delius's seven volume Works of Shakespeare (1854-1860); spelling and punctuation have occasionally been altered to reflect modern usage.

"So how does the book work?"

Shakespeare for Beginners examines the plays first, in roughly the order that we think they were written—we can't be certain. (This book does not include the collaborations, *The Two Noble Kinsmen* and *Henry VIII*.)

This book does not divide the plays into categories (such as comedies, histories, and tragedies), since that approach can be misleading. Shakespeare, himself, did not use any consistent series of labels for the plays he wrote, and pigeonholing them can mean overlooking important parallels between plays that don't happen to fall into the same category.

Shakespeare for Beginners provides summaries of each work, a list of key phrases and themes, brief assessments of main ideas and important concepts in the text, excerpts of key passages, and short but insightful quotes from some of the most influential critics..

Obviously, this book is not meant to replace the works themselves.

And Now, a Brief Word From Our Sponsor

A book summarizing the work of a writer usually suggests that you go out and read the author's books. **Shakespeare for Beginners**, however, will *not* plead with you to read Shakespeare's plays—unless you feel like it. Plays are meant to be *experienced in person*, not read. Dogmatic English instructors force their students to <u>read</u> Shakespeare's plays—then they wonder why the students consider Shakespeare boring.

Any play can be boring if you're forced read it to yourself. A theatrical script is like a roadmap showing the way toward a final work of art—it is not the work of art itself. Plays are designed to be *performed.* If Shakespeare had intended his plays to be read privately rather than acted, he would have seen to it that they were published. As far as we can tell, Shakespeare had no hand in the printing or editing of the dramas he wrote.

If you really want to enjoy Shakespeare's dramatic work, get out to a theater and see a production of the play . . . or rent a good video.

(Or get a bunch of friends together and read the script out loud.)

Once you see the play, you'll have no problem making sense of all of the characters, exits, entrances, and stage directions. But reading a play "cold," dragging yourself through page after page, disoriented and bored—that is an insult to Shakespeare's genius.

The poems, of course, are another matter. They do demand one-on-one attention. Then again, they're probably not what most people think of when they think of Shakespeare!

THE BARD'S HAIR RECONSIDERED:
A CRITICAL STUDY OF INTERPRETATIONS
AS ASSEMBLED BY A TRANS-ATLANTIC
PANEL OF BIOGRAPHICAL RESEARCHERS
SPECIALIZING IN SHAKESPEARE'S
(PURPORTED MALE-PATTERN BALDNESS)

A Few Words About The Bard's Use of Language

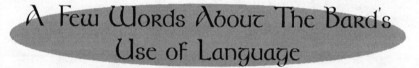

Don't worry if at first you have trouble understanding Shakespeare's language. Everybody does. Then, in no time at all, like listening to a dialect or 'accent' from another part of the country, the fog clears and you wonder why you had any trouble—it's obvious once you get the hang of it. A few helpful 'tricks:'

Again: See the play: A good actor can communicate the meaning of a phrase even when you don't understand the dictionary meaning of each individual word.

Assume (or pretend) that you understand what's being said—and 90% of the time you will.

Stick with it: In no time, you'll run into enough captivating stuff to make you want to "march unto the breach" again and again. Later on, if you like, you can use footnotes and glossaries to your heart's content. A fat encyclopedia could be written about the Bard's verbal style and influence, but this book isn't it.

AND ABOUT BLANK VERSE...

As Shakespeare's career progresses, his proficiency in the ten-syllable blank – that is, unrhyming — verse form becomes breath-taking. (You probably remember blank verse from school: **da-DAH da DAH da DAH da DAH da DAH.**) The Bard's early efforts at verse are often stiff, forced, and monotonous; the middle period shows confident power and expansion; and the final plays demonstrate an amazing ease and fluidity. Look at these examples, which show the change, over two decades, from block-like, self-contained ten-syllable sentences to shifting, smooth-flowing currents of meaning.

📖 **E**arly 1590s: (**Note:** "beldam" means "old hag")

Lay hands upon these traitors and their trash!
Beldam, I think we watch'd you at an inch.
(Henry VI, Part Two, act I, scene iv)

📖 **L**ate 1590s:
You have conspir'd against our royal person,
Join'd with an enemy proclaim'd, and from his coffers
Receiv'd the golden earnest of our death.
(Henry V, act II, scene ii)

📖 **A**round 1610:

But you, my brace of lords, were I so minded,
I here could pluck his Highness' frown upon you
And justify you traitors. At this time
I will tell no tales.
(The Tempest, act V, scene i)

THREE COOL THINGS ABOUT SHAKESPEARE'S ENGLISH

1: When Shakespeare began his career, the English language was flexible and still developing. Shakespeare made the most of the situation, displaying dazzling innovations like a great jazz improviser: Shakespeare turns nouns into verbs, links adjectives together to form new combinations, and borrows words from other languages.

2: Shakespeare's vocabulary is big: 21,000 words plus. Not only can't a modern audience 'understand' every word, Shakespeare's audience couldn't understand every word! Shakespeare often chose his words to *take advantage* of their newness, to make us look at a situation in a new way, and to get the meaning from the context. In other words, he wants you to loosen up and follow him, not sit on each line with a dictionary.

3: Shakespeare often uses what poets call *personification*—giving human attributes to non-humans. In Shakespeare, a tree may be angry, the moon may blush, the morning may have eyes...in most cases, that is not meant to be taken literally—it is *as if the* moon blushed, or *as if the morning had eyes.*

Twenty Words That Will Make
Shakespeare More Accessible

The most dangerous words in Shakespeare aren't the unfamiliar ones, but the ones that seem familiar, but really aren't. They sound straight-forward to our ear, but they carried very different meanings for the audiences of the Bard's day. Here are twenty of the trickiest words you'll find in Shakespeare:

'a: he

an, and: if

awful: capable of inspiring awe

(country name): king or queen (monarchs are often referred to as the nations they lead)

dear: significant, costly

fond: foolish

get: bring into existence

head: army; source

honest: chaste; virtuous; authentic

his: its (Shakespeare hardly ever uses the possessive *its*)

humor: one of the four bodily fluids (choler, blood, phlegm, melancholy) regarded as determining temperament depending on their proportion; mood; outlook

marry: by the Virgin Mary (mild oath)

mere: utter

nice: trifling, silly; fastidious

rub: (as a verb) to strike against something small; (as a noun) an obstacle (both meanings come from bowling, a game that seems to have appealed greatly to Shakespeare)

power: military force

pretend: to intend; to assert; to claim

sad: serious

still: always

tell: to count

There are other deceptive words, of course, but these are some of the most easily mis-understood. As for obviously *unfamiliar* expressions, your best bet, after seeing a performance of the play, is to track down a good annotated text of the play in question.

In his best moments, Shakespeare is *alive*, more alive, perhaps, than any other writer who's ever lived. But don't take my word for it— see for yourself.

And now, on with the show . . .

Two Gentlemen of Verona

WHERE LIES THE SCENE?

Verona and Milan, and a forest close to Mantua.

WHAT HAPPENS?

Two friends, **Valentine** and **Proteus**, the gentlemen of the title, prepare to take their leave of each other. Valentine is bound for the court of the **Duke of Milan**; Proteus, in love with **Julia**, will stay in Verona in hopes of winning her affections. Upon arriving in Milan, Valentine meets and falls in love with **Silvia**, the Duke's daughter. Proteus, having himself been ordered to Milan by his father, learns from Valentine that he (Valentine) and Silvia, are planning to elope — inasmuch as the Duke wishes Silvia to wed the wealthy dolt **Thurio**. Valentine asks for his friend's help in arranging things. The problem: Proteus has fallen instantly in love with Silvia. Julia, still in Verona and unaware of Proteus's newfound passion in Milan, leaves disguised as a boy, hoping to find him Proteus tells the Duke of Milan about Valentine's plan to escape with Silvia and get married. Valentine is banished. Proteus pretends to help Thurio win the affections of Silvia. A band of outlaws captures Valentine and names him as their leader. Julia arrives, in disguise, from Verona. After surmising what Proteus is up to, she wins a place in his service by pretending to be a boy. Julia, acting as Proteus's page, is sent to bestow a gift on Silvia — a ring that Julia had given to

Proteus. Silvia refuses it. Silvia makes her escape from Milan and sets out to join Valentine. She is apprehended by members of the wandering band of outlaws, but Proteus and his "page" rescue her. Proteus proves himself once and for all to be a cad and a bounder by preparing to force himself on Silvia, but Valentine, who has been hiding himself nearby, intervenes. In one of the strangest moments in all of Shakespeare, Valentine accepts his friend's apology, then offers him his beloved, Silvia. Julia, disguised as the page, swoons. Thanks to a ring she is wearing, her true identity is discovered. She, too, forgives Proteus for no discernable reason. The Duke materializes, having been taken prisoner by the forest outlaws. He grants a pardon to anyone in need of one and gives his blessing to the love of Valentine and Silvia. Both couples live happily ever after.

KEEP AN EAR OUT FOR ONGOING REFERENCES TO . . . Friendship and love, animals, duty and service.

WHAT'S IT ALL ABOUT?

Some scholars feel The Two Gentlemen of Verona to be a strong candidate as Shakespeare's first piece of professional playwriting. If it isn't the Bard's first effort, it is certainly one of his earliest pieces of dramatic work, and it shows. Although certain elements of the play are echoed in other memorable comedies of his — the potentially all-consuming nature of love, the constancy of young women in love when compared to the young men who pursue them, the device of an ingenue's assuming the guise of a young boy — these are not handled with quite the same poise and precision as elsewhere. Truth be told, the play has all the hallmarks of an apprentice work. The Two Gentlemen of Verona, although it boasts high moments from such characters as the loving Julia and the plain-spoken clown Launce, is neither a particularly strong piece of writing nor a very funny comedy. It's generally considered an early foray into areas that would be traveled more profitably later in the writer's career.

LINES TO LISTEN FOR

I have no other but a woman's reason: I think him so, because I think him so. (I, ii)

O hateful hands, to tear such loving words!
Injurious wasps, to feed on such sweet honey,
    And kill the bees that yield it with your stings! (I, ii)

Methinks my zeal to Valentine is cold,
    And that I love him not as I was wont:
        O, but I love his lady too too much,
            And that's the reason I love him so little. (II, iv)

Time is the nurse and breeder of all good. (III, i)

I'll force thee yield to my desire! (V, iv)

All that was mine in Silvia I give thee. (V, iv)

THE CRITICS' CORNER

"It is the general opinion that (**The Two Gentlemen of Verona**) abounds with weeds, and there is no one, I think, will deny, who peruses it with attention, that it is adorned with several poetical flowers such as the hand of a Shakespeare alone could have raised." **(Benjamin Victor)**

"In this play there is a strange mixture of knowledge and ignorance of care and negligence." **(Samuel Johnson)**

"When it is true to itself the comedy insists on both the importance and the relativity of love." **(Anne Barton)**

Some cool things about ❈ The Two Gentlemen of Verona ❈

5: Launce's scenes may have been added on after a preliminary draft of the play was completed.

4: Julia's assumption of a male disguise is a device that appears in a number of the later comedies; since the ingenue roles were played by boys on the Elizabethan stage, there must have been an air of realism to the "disguise"!

3: The play features a number of strange inconsistencies: sea voyages to towns that shouldn't require them, varying titles for Silvia's father (Duke? Emperor?), and an unsettling lack of certainty about the settings of some of the scenes.

2: The sublime worthiness of true friendship between two men, and the superiority of that friendship to the love between a man and a woman, was a common theme in the literature of Elizabethan England. Maybe the bizzarre ending was a little less bizzarre to Shakespeare's audience than it is to us. Then again, maybe not.

1: This play, which scholars estimate was written and performed in the early 1590's, was not published until the First Folio of 1623. By all indications, it was not a great popular success.

> DID I NOT BID THEE STILL MARK ME, AND DO AS I DO? WHEN DIDST THOU SEE ME HEAVE UP MY LEG AND MAKE WATER AGAINST A GENTLEWOMAN'S FARTHINGALE? DIDST THOU EVER SEE ME DO SUCH A TRICK?

> Geez, I can't wait until the fire hydrant is invented.

HENRY VI
PARTS I, II & III

WHERE LIES THE SCENE?

Fifteenth-century England and France

WHAT HAPPENS?

PART ONE:

The triumphant conquerer **Henry V** has died; his youthful successor, Henry VI, assumes the throne. The disputed English holdings in France are reported lost. The **Earl of Salisbury**, accompanied by **Lord Talbot** and his son **John Talbot**, fight bravely against the French at Orleans. Salisbury is killed. A sheperdess, **Joan La Pucelle** (Joan of Arc), appealing to divine visions, rallies the French and claims Orleans. Young King Henry's troubled reign begins as self-serving uncles assume his authority and mismanage the kingdom. Foreign and domestic turmoil marks the king's early tenure. During the celebration that follows the French military action at Orleans, the English launch an assault and reassume control of the city. The rival houses of **York** and **Lancaster**, represented by white and red roses, respectively, initiate the rancorous quarrel that will become the *Wars of the Roses*, a long and bloody period of civil discord that will bear out the dark prophecy made by the Bishop of Carlisle upon the deposition of **Richard II** by **Henry**

17

Bolingbroke. **Richard Plantagenet**, of the house of York (who has learned from his dying uncle that he is the true heir to Richard II) and **John Beaufort**, Earl of Somerset, of the house of Lancaster, emerge as the the major figures in the dispute between the two sides Attempts to quell the increasingly bitter disputes between the two sides result in Plantagenet's being named the Duke of York. The young king sees the disaster unfolding in his kingdom, but can do nothing to prevent it The French assume control of Rouen, only to lose it back to the English. Henry is crowned for the second time at Paris. The king's latest pleas for domestic peace go unheded. Talbot and his son die during the English attempt to take Bordeaux. A truce between the English and the French is arranged; it is to be confirmed by the young king's marriage to the daughter of the **Earl of Armagnac**. At Angiers, Joan is taken prisoner by the English and burned as a witch. King Henry, swayed by the Earl of Suffolk's description of **Margaret of Anjou**, resolves to marry her instead.

PART TWO:

We learn that the King's marriage to Margaret carries with it no dowry, and requires the King to yield the duchies of Anjou and Maine. Although the worthy **Duke of Gloucester** has his doubts about the union, the King goes forward with it. Gloucester's ambitious wife **Eleanor**, the duchess, falls into a trap set for her by rival nobles, and is arrested as a traitor. **Richard Plantagenet**, Duke of York, convinces the earls of Warwick and Salisbury of the soundness of his claim to the throne. The Duchess of Gloucester is banished. Her shattered husband does not dispute the sentence, but instead resigns. The King is thus deprived of the only honest voice in his court. The Duke of Suffolk follows the Queen's lead and has the blameless Gloucester arrested for treason.

Gloucester is not convicted of any crime, however; when Gloucester's corpse is produced by the Earl of Warwick, Suffolk is banished. The rival houses again mar the peace with their quarrelling. King Henry sends his increasingly restless rival Richard Plantagenet to Ireland. A popular rebellion is incited by **Jack Cade**, a fast-talking rabble-rouser. **Lord Clifford** skilfully turns the gathered citizens against their leader. Plantagenet returns from Ireland, having raised an army. Henry tries to assuage him by sending a delegate promising to imprison Plantagenet's chief Lancastrian rival, Somerset, but the promise is not carried out, and the forces of the house of York are before too long arrayed directly against the king. The Lancastrians align with the king, and the two forces meet on the battlefield. Plantagenet's forces carry the day; his crook-backed son, also named Richard, kills his father's rival Somerset. King Henry flees. England is in utter chaos.

a rose may not be a rose maynot be a rose.

PART THREE:

The King arrives in London only to find Richard of York occupying his throne in Parliament — and supported by the powerful Earl of Warwick. Henry feebly begs to be allowed to occupy the throne until his death, and agrees to name Richard as his successor. He is allowed to resume the throne, but his queen, Margaret, is incensed at the news of the King's capitulation and swears to raise a force against the House of York. Richard Plantagenet's sons — Edward and the hunchbacked Richard — convince him to renege on his agreement with Henry and assume the throne at once. However, in a battle against the army led by Margaret and supported by Lord Clifford, the forces of York are defeated, and Richard Plantagenet's head is set above the gates of York. Plantagenet's sons Edward and Richard resolve to continue the fight, and are joined by the recently defeated Warwick. The two sides once again engage in a bloody battle. This time the forces fighting in support of the weak-willed (and disengaged) king are defeated. Lord Clifford is beheaded. Edward of York is crowned as King Edward IV. The deposed king, who has been hiding in Scotland, returns for a glimpse of the land he loves. He is encountered by a pair of gamekeepers who turn him over to the authorities. Henry is dispatched to the Tower of London. The new king, Edward, falls in love with the widowed Lady Grey. The deformed Richard begins scheming for the crown. Warwick, in France attemptingto engineer a marriage with the daughter of the French king that will secure Edward's claim to the crown, is furious to learn that his king has married Lady Grey. He aligns himself with the deposed Queen Margaret, and secures the support of the French king in reinstating Henry. · The sons of the slain Richard Plantagenet, one of whom is the King of England, cannot make common cause against the force that is advancing against them; **Clarence**, brother to Edward and Richard, joins forces with Warwick and the French. The invading army deprives Edward of the crown and returns Henry to the throne. Edward escapes from his captivity and heads an army of his own; he throws Henry back into the imprisonment of the Tower and reclaims the crown. In the ensuing battle against Warwick, Clarence refuses to fight against his brothers. Warwick dies. Margaret, attempting to reinforce Warwick's force, is overcome and imprisoned. The deposed king's son is murdered. The evil Richard, Duke of Gloucester, makes his way to the Tower and finds Henry placidly reading a book; Richard kills him. Margaret's father ransoms her. Edward secures the throne. The bloodthirsty and ambitious Richard awaits his own chance to claim the crown.

KEEP AN EAR OUT FOR ONGOING REFERENCES TO ...

Gardens and orchards, weeds, trees; traps **(in Part One)**; butchers and slaughterhouses **(in Parts Two and Three)**; chaos and storms **(in Part Three)**.

Virtually everything is up front in this early group of history plays. For the most part, characterizations are simple (and occasionally crude), ambiguity is minimal or nonexistent, and psychological insight takes a back seat to action and the forward movement of the massive plot. The story-line focuses on **the fall of Talbot (Part One)**, **the rise of the Yorkists** (Part Two) **and the ever-intensifying holcaust of the civil war** (Part Three). Henry VI is eclipsed by Talbot in Part One, seems peripheral in Part Two, and is finally overwhelmed by large and dark forces far more interesting than he is in Part Three. The fascinating "foul undigested lump" Richard, who becomes Duke of Gloucester in Part Three, will emerge as an audience-grabbing protagonist to be reckoned with in *Richard III*.

The authorship of these three early plays has been the subject of intense conjecture. Most scholars now accept his leading role in the creation of the trilogy.

THE CRITICS' CORNER

"This is the last and loftiest farewell not of rhyming tragedy; still in in King Richard II and in Romeo and Juliet it struggles for a while to keep its footing, but now more visibly in vain."
(Algernon Charles Swinburne)

"Repeatedly, the question of Henry's right to rule turns on the the question of whether he can rule." **(Moody E. Prior)**

"The Wars of the Roses snowball from a private dispute between individuals in *King Henry VI Part One* into a conflict which, tears apart families, social classes, ultimately the nation itself . . ."
(Levi Fox)

LINES TO LISTEN FOR

Glory is like a circle in the water,
Which never ceaseth to enlarge itself,
Till by broad spreading it disperse to nought.
(Part One, I, ii)

. . . here I prophesy:
this brawl to-day
Grown to this faction in the
Temple Garden
Shall send, between the Red Rose
and the White,
A thousand souls to death
and deadly night. (Part
One, II, iv)

The fraud of
England, not the
force of France,
Hath now entrapp'd the noble-
minded Talbot.
Never to England shall he
bear his life,
But dies betray'd to fortune
by your strife. (Part
One, IV, iv)

O peers of England, shameful is this league!
Fatal this marriage, cancelling your fame,
Blotting your names from books of memory,
Raising the characters of your renown,
Defacing monuments of conquer'd France,
Undoing all as all had never been.
(Part Two, I,i)

Unbidden
guests are often
welcomest when
they are gone.
(Part One, II,
ii)

. . . let my head
Stoop to the block than these
knees bow to any
Save to the God of heaven and to
my king. (Part Two, IV, i)

Could I come near your beauty
with my nails
I'd set my ten commandments in
your face. (Part Two, I, iii)

Of all base pas-
sions, fear is most
accurs'd.
(Part One, V, ii)

The first thing we do, let's kill all
the lawyers. (Part Two, IV, ii)

O tiger's heart wrapp'd in a woman's hide! (Part Three, I, iv)

King. Good Margaret, stay.
Queen: What are you made of? You'll nor fight nor fly. (Part Two, V, ii)

Cade: . . . I charge and command that, of the city's cost, the pissing-conduit run nothing but claret wine this first year of our reign. (Part Two, IV, vi)

And many strokes, though with a little axe, Hew down and fell the hardest-timber'd oak. (Part Three, II, i)

A little fire is quickly trodden out; Which, being suffered, rivers cannot quench. (Part Three, IV, viii)

Then, since the heavens have shap'd my body so, Let hell make crook'd my mind to answer it. I have no brother, I am like no brother; And this word "love," which greybeards call divine, Be resident in men like one another, And not in me! I am myself alone. (Part Three, V, vi)

Every cloud engenders not a storm. (Part Three, V, iii)

Thus yields the cedar to the axe's edge. (Part Three, V, ii)

This shoulder was ordain'd so thick to heave, And heave it shall some weight, or break my back. (Part Three, V, vii)

The smallest worm will turn, being trodden on. (Part Three, II, ii)

25

SOME COOL THINGS ABOUT HENRY VI

5: In Part One, Talbot's death speech (act IV, scene vii), delivered while he holds his dead son in his arms, is a prime example of Shakespeare's early style.

4: In Part Two, the rebellion led by Jack Cade (beginning in act IV, scene ii) highlights the emerging distinction between irreverent, streetwise prose ("There shall be in England seven halfpenny loaves sold for a penny," Cade boasts) and formal verse (The king laments, "O graceless men! They know not what they do!").

3: Henry's speech yearning for the life of a humble shepherd (Part Three, act II, scene v) prefigures memorable speeches by both Richard II and Henry V on the relative lots of subjects and kings.

4: In Part Three, the cunning Richard emerges as a malignant force to be reckoned with. See his speech beginning "Why, I can smile, and murther [murder] whiles I smile," in act III, scene ii.

1: The political and military chaos of Part Three is symbolized by storm imagery, a comparison that will recur in more mature form in later plays.

RICHARD THE THIRD

WHERE LIES THE SCENE?

Late fifteeth-century Britain.

WHAT HAPPENS?

Richard, the deformed **Duke of Gloucester**, is out to attain the English crown by any means necessary. By playing upon the superstitions of the ailing King Edward IV, Richard turns the king against **George, Duke of Clarence** — brother to the king, and Richard's own older brother. Richard woos **Lady Anne**, whose father and husband he he has killed, and somehow convinces her that he undertook his actions out of love for her. Richard is settled upon as Protector of the young sons of **Edward IV. Clarence**, confined to the Tower of London, has a harrowing dream, and is murdered by the agents of his brother. Edward IV dies. Young Prince Edward is summoned to be crowned. With the help of his ally **Buckingham**, Richard imprisons the supporters of **Queen Elizabeth**. Richard manages to attain control of both of the Queen's sons and, pretending that his is making ready for the coronation of the Prince, places both boys in the Tower of London. Through one of his men, Richard sounds out Lord Hastings on his support for Richard's ascension to the throne. Hastings continues to support the young Prince; at a later meeting, Richard makes a fantastic charge of treason against Hastings and orders him executed. Other of the Prince's supporters are murdered; Buckingham engineers popular support for Richard after spreading malicious rumors about the old King and his family. The Lord Mayor of London, accompanied by a crowd of citizens, beseeches the "reluctant" Richard to assume the crown. Richard arranges for the murders of the two sons of Elizabeth. Buckingham senses that Richard is likely to turn on him, too, and determines to join the party of Henry Richmond, in opposition to Richard. Having set out rumors that his wife Anne was gravely ill, and having then arranged for her death, Richard suggests himself as a husband to the niece of Queen Elizabeth, who is betrothed to Richmond. A huge army under the command of Richmond lands and attracts the support of key noblemen. Buckingham is captured and executed. · Richard's forces prepare to confront Richmond's; the night before the battle, Richard is visited in a dream by the many victims of his treachery. Although he shows great courage in the battle, Richard is slain by Richmond himself, who assumes the throne as Henry VII.

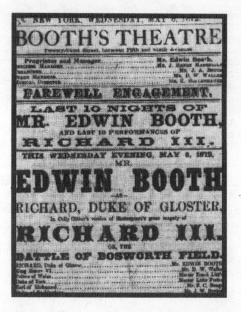

The uncertain structure, simplistic characterizations, and incident-crammed story-lines of the three **Henry VI** plays resolve in a surprisingly confident style — and a dominating central character. **Richard III**, the fourth and final play in the series, is about one man and the havoc he wreaks on England. The play is a pageant (and often a surprisingly funny one) of ruthless ambition. Although we in the audience know that Richard must fall, we also take a secret delight in his unrelenting, inventive immorality. We want to see him punished — but not too soon. This skillfully evoked divided interest in a morally reprehensible person will resurface when we see Shylock **(in The Merchant of Venice)**, Falstaff **(in the Henry IV plays)**, Iago **(in Othello)**, and Regan, Goneril, and Edmund **(in King Lear)**. All of these fascinating but ultimately destructive people meet with very unhappy ends indeed. They claim as their "father" the brilliant, hunchbacked maneuverer Richard, Shakespeare's first great character study.

Keep an ear out for ongoing references to:

Gardens and orchards, trees, animals.

Speech bubble: NOW IS THE WINTER OF OUR DISCONTENT MADE GLORIOUS SUMMER BY THIS SUN OF YORK. (I, i)

The Critic's Corner

"Crimes are (Richard's) delight: but Macbeth is always in an agony when he thinks of them." (Thomas Whately)

"The . . hump, the conscience, the fear of ghosts, all impart a spice of outrageousness which leaves nothing lacking to the fun of the entertainment, except the solemnity of those spectators who feel bound to take the affair as a profound and subtle historic study." (George Bernard Shaw)

"There is another peculiarity of the present drama which ought to be mentioned — the frequent use of the curse. It is a terrific weapon, and it is employed here with terrific violence." (Denton J. Snider)

Simple plain Clarence! I do love thee so
That I will shortly send thy soul to heaven . . . (I, i)

Was ever woman in this humour woo'd?
Was ever woman in this humour won? (I, ii)

Talkers are not good doers. (I, iii)

I am not in the giving vein today. (IV, ii)

So now prosperity begins to mellow
And drop into the rotten mouth of death. (IV, iv)

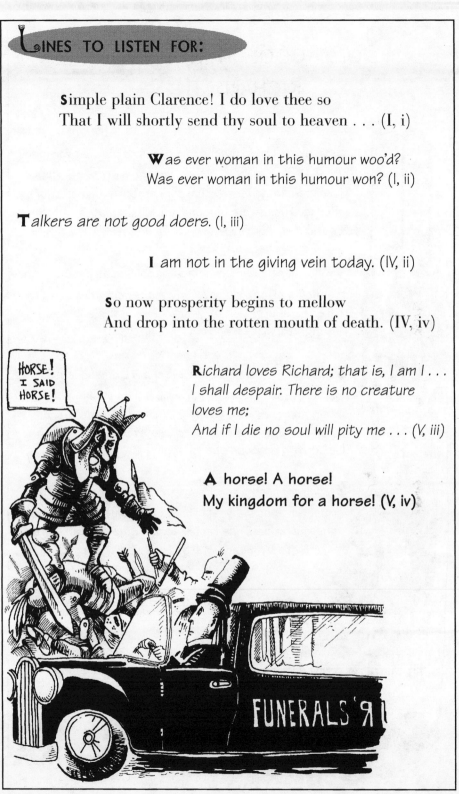

HORSE!
I SAID
HORSE!

Richard loves Richard; that is, I am I . . .
I shall despair. There is no creature
loves me;
And if I die no soul will pity me . . . (V, iii)

A horse! A horse!
My kingdom for a horse! (V, iv)

FUNERALS 'Я

Some cool things about Richard III:

5: Shakespeare's main source for the play, as for many of the English history plays, was the historian Raphael Holinshed. In addition, Shakespeare's (strongly Tudor-influenced) portrait of Richard took a great deal from Sir Thomas More's *History of Richard the Third*.

4: The ruthless ambition and quasi-Satanic moral code ascribed by Shakespeare to Richard were intended to make the usurpation of Henry VII — grandfather of Queen Elizabeth — seem necessary.

3: Modern-day defenders of Richard are eloquent in their protests that the portrait of him in this play is unfair, and they are probably justified — but all the same, the play has convinced people for centuries that the Yorkist king was the embodiment of evil.

2: *Richard III* shows off some of Shakespeare's early, formal verse at its best. The remarkable scene in which the king woos Anne (act I, scene ii) gains many of its effects by means of its clever use of parallel, almost sing-song constructions.

I. In the play, Clarence dies after Richard is named Protector; in reality, Clarence died five years beforehand. Here and elswhere, Shakespeare took a liberal approach to adapting history.

The Comedy of Errors

Where lies the scene?
Ancient Ephesus

What happens?

The rivalry between cities of **Ephesus** and **Syracuse** leads **Solinus**, the Duke of Ephesus, to condemn to death an old merchant from Syracuse, **Aegeon** by name, who has entered Ephosus. Aegeon pleads for his life, explaining his sad history. Years ago, he bought, as servants, twin infant sons who would, he hoped, eventually care for his own recently-born twin boys. During a sea voyage, however, Aegeon and his wife were separated; the wife rescued one of her sons and one of the tiny slaves, and Aegeon himself rescued the other pair of infants. Aegeon witnessed the rescue of his wife and the two babies by a boat owned by Corinthian fishermen; he himself was rescued by another vessel and conveyed to **Epidaurus**. Aegeon explains that, after eighteen years, he gave his son and his son's slave permission to depart Syracuse and search for the long-lost brother. After some time passed with no word from his son, Aegeon himself set out on a long search; five years passed, but with no luck. It was while attempting to return to his home in Syracuse that Aegeon was apprehended by the authorities at Ephesus. The Duke grants Aegeon a single day to meet his ransom. Otherwise, he must face death. The very son Aegeon set out to find, **Antipholus of Syracuse**, has recently come to Ephesus, claiming to be from another town in order to avoid the penalty awaiting any person from Syracuse who sets foot in Ephesus. Antipholus of Syracuse, ignorant of his father's presence in Ephesus, is also unaware that his long-lost brother has set up house in this town. Each brother is named Antipholus; each has a slave named Dromio. Each set of twins is, of course, identical. A series of complex misadventures ensues, based on the confusion of the various brothers' (and their slaves') identities. Is it witch-craft in Ephesus that caus-es complete strangers to act in such a familiar way — and make such strange accu-sations against the young men? In the end, the pairs of brothers are reunited, Aegeon is pardoned, and his wife, the mother of the Antipholuses, is rediscovered.

WHAT'S IT ALL ABOUT?

The Comedy of Errors may lack the insight of such later comedies as *Much Ado About Nothing* and *Twelfth Night*, but it is still expertly assembled, and a supremely stageworthy piece of work. The job at hand here is to get laughs, and the Bard sets about getting them with a confident hand. (Compare the similarly well-structured, if not particularly profound, blood tragedy *Titus Andronicus*, another early effort that adopts a Roman theme.) Old Aegeon's death sentence at the play's outset, although unlikely to be a cause of much real concern to a theatergoing audience, incorporates a threat of death that will be overcome by the action of the play. This parallels similar triumphs over representations of Death in later comedies: The play-within-a-play of *A Midsummer Night's Dream,* for instance, or Shylock's demand for a pound of flesh in *The Merchant of Venice.*

❧ THE CRITICS'S CORNER ❧

"(The play) invites compassion, a measure of sympathy, and a deeper response to the disruption of social and family which the action brings about." (R.A. Foakes).

"In style, **The Comedy of Errors** is a microcosm of early Shakespeare: the frequent rhymes, the end-stopped lines, the quibbles, the rhetorical dialectic of question and answer in a single speech . . . all are there." (Marion Bodwell Smith.)

Proceed, Solinus, to procure my fall, And by the doom of death end woes and all. (I, i)

How comes it now, my husband, O, how comes it, That thou art then estranged from thyself? (II, ii)

I TO THE WORLD AM LIKE A DROP OF WATER, THAT IN THE OCEAN SEEKS ANOTHER DROP. (I, ii)

She is spherical, like a globe; I could find out countries in her. (III, ii)

Stay, stand apart — I know not which is which. (V, i)

Some cool things about The Comedy of Errors

5: It is the shortest of all of Shakespeare's plays.

4: The comedy is based on two plays by Plautus, the **Menaechmi** and the **Amphitruo.**

3: The 1938 Rodgers and Hart musical **The Boys from Syracuse** was inspired by **The Comedy of Errors.**

2: Act III, scene 2 features an amusing passage of bawdy (and anachronistic) geographical wordplay, in which Dromio of Syracuse anatomizes his portly ladyfriend Nell.

1: At least one modern production has creatively overcome the problem of finding "identical" actors to play the twins, who must appear onstage together simultaneously. The producers cast a black actor in one of the roles and a white actor in the other!

TITUS ANDRONICUS

WHERE LIES THE SCENE?
Ancient Rome

WHAT HAPPENS?

Titus returns home to Rome, having defeated the Goths. The vanquished **Queen Tamora** pleads for the life of one of her three sons, **Alarbus**; nevertheless, he is offered in sacrifice. Titus refuses the throne in deference to **Saturninus**, the dead emperor's elder son. Titus' consents to Saturninus's request for the hand of Titus's daughter **Lavinia** in marriage. Saturninus's brother **Bassianus**, claims that Lavinia has agreed to marry him. Bassianus, and Lavinia's own brothers, kidnap her in order to keep the marriage from taking place. Titus attempts to pursue the men, but his son **Mutius** bars his way. Titus kills him. Saturninus chooses to marry **Tamora**. Bassianus is murdered by Tamora's sons after observing her with her Moorish lover, **Aaron**; Lavinia is raped by the queen's sons, and to make certainty of her silence, her tongue is torn out and her hands cut off. Titus's sons Martius and Quintus are falsely accused of Bassianus's murder and sentenced to death; their brother Lucius is banished. The evil Aaron informs Titus that the Emperor will spare the lives of the young men if Titus, his brother Marcus, or the banished Lucius will cut off a hand and have it sent to the Emperor. Titus dutifully cuts off his hand and forwards it to the Emperor; it is returned, along with the heads of his sons. Titus sends Lucius away to raise a military force. · Using a stick held between her stumps, Lavinia identifies her assailants. Titus pretends to be mad. · Tamora gives birth to a child. Aaron is the father. Aaron kills the child's nurse, makes arrangements for a white baby to be acknowledged as the Emperor's son, and departs to raise his son among the Goths. Lucius and his army of Goths begin their march on Rome. Tamora arranges to meet with Titus, hoping to take advantage of his (supposedly) distracted state and win his aid in separating Lucius from his forces. When she and her sons arrive at Titus's house, Titus appears to be taken in by her tricks. When the opportunity arises, however, he kills her sons, bakes them in a pie, and, ultimately, serves them to the Emperor and Empress at a formal banquet. A culminating spasm of mayhem sees Titus murder his own daughter ("and with thy shame thy father's sorrow die"); Titus stab Tamora; Saturnius slay Titus; and Lucius vanquish Saturninus.

EXHIBIT B

EXHIBIT A

WHAT'S IT ALL ABOUT?

This shallowly conceived bloodbath has provoked two extreme (and contradictory) reactions from Shakespearean critics over the centuries. One camp holds that the piece is so luridly disgusting, and such an affront to the later works of the playwright, that it cannot have been written by him in first place. Another camp (more likely to be made up of modern critics) accepts Shakespeare's authorship of the play, and tries to trace out the deep meaning and profound thematic resonance found in later plays. (For instance, the idea that Rome itself is metaphorically "dismembered" by a corrupt moral order, and that the conclusion shows a hard-won return to wholeness.) Both views of the play are incomplete. A successful modern-day screenwriter may not be particularly proud of his hand in creating *Killer Co-Eds Part Six*, but he may very well, in his most honest moments, admit that he learned something about dramatic structure by writing a crowd-pleasing piece of sensationalism. That's what *Titus Andronicus* is. If this play fails to deliver the deep insights and the sense of moral purgation of later tragedies, it still shows off a rapidly maturing set of technical skills and the ability to hold the attention of an audience.

KEEP AN EAR OUT FOR ONGOING REFERENCES TO . . .
Animals, hunting, revenge.

LINES TO LISTEN FOR

What, villain boy, Barr'st me my way in Rome?
(Titus's words before killing his son Mutius.) (I, i)

> **S**he is a woman, therefore may be woo'd;
> She is a woman, therefore may be won.
> She is Lavinia, therefore must be lov'd. (II, i)

Why dost not speak to me?
Alas, a crimson river of warm blood,
Like to a bubbling fountain stirr'd with wind,
Doth rise and fall between thy rosed lips,
Coming and going with thy honey breath. (II, iv)

⊕ft have I digg'd up dead men from their graves,
And set them upright at their dear friends' door,
Even when their sorrows almost was forgot. (V, i)

> **I**f one good deed in all my life I did,
> I do repent it from my very soul. (V, iii)

41

Some cool things about Titus Andronicus

5: The most authoritative text for the vast majority of play was not discovered until 1904. But this text does not supply . . .

4: . . . act II, scene ii, in which Titus upbraids Marcus for killing a fly, then whacks away at it himself. This scene appears only in the 1623 Folio version.

3: One of history's most disgusting stage directions appears in act II, scene iv: "Enter . . . Lavinia, her hands cut off, and her tongue cut out, and ravish'd."

2: During the author's lifetime, Titus Andronicus was apparently one of Shakespeare's most popular plays.

1: Playwright Ben Jonson made fun of Titus Andronicus in his 1614 play Bartholemew Fair.

42

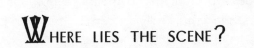

SHREW WHO?

The Taming of the Shrew

WHERE LIES THE SCENE?

In Padua, and in the country house of Petruchio.

WHAT HAPPENS?

In the Induction, a drunken tinker by the name of **Christopher Sly** is found by a nobleman. The tinker is conveyed to a room in the nobleman's castle and dressed in fine clothing; when he wakes up, he is surrounded by servants and informed that he is a lord who has just recovered from fifteen years of insanity. Ostensibly in order to keep Sly's mood up and avoid further mental trauma, a troupe of actors perform the comedy *The Taming of the Shrew*. A wealthy merchant, **Baptista Minola of Padua**, has two daughters: **Katherina**, who is possessed of a violent temper, and her younger sister **Bianca**, who is docile and obliging. Baptista insists that the older sister must be married before he will consent to the marriage of the younger. Petruchio, a plain-spoken gentleman of Verona, resolves to claim Katherina and the healthy dowry Baptista is offering any man brave enough to wed her. In wooing her, Petruchio is aiding the cause of the suitors of Bianca — **Lucentio** (who has assumed a false identity as a tutor in order to see Bianca), **Hortensio**, and **Gremio**. Claiming to hear only sweetness in

Katherina's ceaseless torrent of insults, Petruchio sets a wedding date. The rival wooers of Bianca engage in a series of attempts to win her hand. Petruchio arranges a number of absurd humiliations for Katherina: on their wedding day, he arrives late and dressed in ludicrous clothing. He behaves outrageously during the ceremony and, before she can enjoy the bridal feast, conveys his bride home on an old, distinctly unimpressive horse. Katherina receives more strange treatment when she arrives at Petruchio's country house. Petruchio will not allow her to eat or sleep, claiming that the food and bed are unworthy of her. These and other examples of surrealistic misconduct on Petruchio's part begin to wear Katherina down. By the time the two return to Baptista's home, Katherina's outlook has changed markedly. Lucentio has won Bianca; Hortensio has found a widow to marry. As the play nears its conclusion, the three new husbands place a bet: Whose wife will prove the most obedient? Petruchio is the winner of the wager.

Keep an ear out for ongoing references to . . .

Pride, bluster, roughness, duty, appearance.

❧ Wʜᴀᴛ's ɪᴛ ᴀʟʟ ᴀʙᴏᴜᴛ? ❧

Even critics of the piece's "attitude toward women" generally admit
that **The Taming of the Shrew** gives less offense in performance than it
does when read silently — which it was never meant to be. Although it's
set firmly and predictably in its Elizabethan world-view of the proper relations between men and women, *The Taming of the Shrew* is more a play of
reconciliation than one of sexism. Sad but true: Katherina is a supremely
selfish person when we first meet her. Petruchio's unorthodox treatment
of her is meant only to illustrate to her, in a dramatic way, the difficulty
of living in the company of a person who takes complete, and usually
rather arbitrary, self-centeredness as a guiding philosopy. The gambit
works. Katherina learns to let go of her harsh persona — and it is only a
persona — and finds herself able to show concern for someone other
than herself. **The Taming of the Shrew** is replete with ideas of disguise,
role-playing, and transformation, both in the main plot and the supporting story of Bianca and her suitors. The play seems to be saying that the
many masks men and women wear in their dealings with one another are
unavoidable, but that they sometimes get in the way of healthy relationships.

> HAVE I NOT IN A PITCHED BATTLE HEARD LOUD 'LARUMS, NEIGHING STEEDS, AND TRUMPETS CLANG?
> AND DO YOU TELL ME OF A WOMAN'S TONGUE, THAT GIVES NOT HALF SO GREAT A BLOW TO HEAR AS WILL A CHESTNUT IN A FARMER'S FIRE?
> TUSH, TUSH, FEAR BOYS WITH BUGS.
> (I, ii)

LINES TO LISTEN FOR

> Such duty as the subject owes the prince,
> Even such a woman oweth her husband . . . (V, ii)

> He that is giddy thinks the world turns round. (V, ii)

> Then God be bless'd, it is the blessed sun!
> But sun it is not when you say it is not,
> And the moon changes even as your mind.
> (IV, v)

> I will be master of what is mine own.
> She is my goods, my chattels; she is my house,
> My household stuff, my field, my barn,
> My horse, my ox, my ass, my anything,
> And here she stands. Touch her whoever dare. (III, ii)

THE CRITICS' CORNER

"No man with any decency of feeling can sit it out in the company of a woman without feeling extremely ashamed of the lord-of-creation moral implied in the wager and the speech put into the woman's own mouth." (George Bernard Shaw)

"(The play is) a dramatic exploration of the nature of role playing in comedy and in life." (Richard Henze)

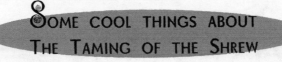
5: In drawing Katherina as a relatively complex human being, rather than a one-note puppet, Shakespeare chose to depart from the many coarse depictions and accounts of "shrews" common in his time.

4: The inexplicable disappearance of the Christopher Sly thread after his appearance in the Induction has given rise to a good deal of (inconclusive) scholarly debate. Most productions delete the Induction; a few insert scenes from an anonymous contemporary play dealing with the same story that features, puzzlingly, a fully-executed "frame" to the play within a play.

3: Katherina's broadly drawn battles with Petruchio prefigure the exquisite verbal warfare of Beatrice and Benedick in the later play *Much Ado About Nothing.*

2: Around 1611, the playwright John Fletcher wrote a sequel, *The Woman's Prize, or the Tamer Tamed,* in which the widowed Petruchio is himself tamed by his next wife.

1: Although it is not a favorite of the scholarly crowd, *The Taming of the Shrew* has been a consistently reliable audience draw for over four hundred years.

WHERE LIES THE SCENE?
Navarre

WHAT HAPPENS?

King Ferdinand of Navarre and his three noble friends
Berowne, Longaville, and **Dumain** have sworn to spend three
years together in earnest study, away from the sight of
women. The princess of France arrives to discuss diplomatic
matters. She brings three three ladies — **Rosaline, Maria,**
and **Katherine** — with her. Before long the king has become
captivated by the princess, and his three friends with the
ladies of her company. **Armado**, a verbose Spaniard, falls in
love with the wench **Jaquenetta** and sends her a love letter.
Berowne sends a letter to Rosaline. The clown **Costard** gets
the letters mixed up and delivers them to the wrong parties.
The king, Longaville, and Dumain have all been pining after their
respective loves; Berowne makes fun of them, but is interrupted by the return of his own love letter. The men realize how
absurd their attempt to exclude women from their lives was,
and arrange an entertainment at the Princess's pavilion. The
women are wise to the scheme of the men, who have disguised

themselves as Russians. The masked ladies at the dance are wooed by the wrong men. In time, they reveal themselves, and make it clear that they are enjoying a joke at the expense of their suitors. A pageant presented by Costard, Sir Nathaniel, Holofernes, Moth, and Armado, representing the Nine Worthies, is presented; the king and his companions mock the performers. A messenger brings news that the King of France — father to the princess — has died. The king asks the princess to marry him, and requests the hands of her three ladies for his three courtiers. The lovers do not unite; the wary women promise to respond to the proposal after a year and a day of mourning has passed.

Keep an ear out for ongoing references to . . .

War, weapons, battle, games.

OW!

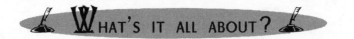
No happy ending here! *Love's Labour's Lost* features more cautious circling around ideas, people, and carefully preplanned events than actual "incident," and in some ways is more reminiscent of the drawn-out, verbally dense *Hamlet* than of the other comedies. The overall tone of the piece, however, is not that of *Hamlet*. This is a dazzling showcase of wit, poetry, and parody — or at any rate, it was a dazzling showcase of wit, poetry, and parody for the audience for which it was intended. Modern viewers are likely to be intimidated by the seemingly endless topical references and multilayered linguistic conceits based firmly in the Elizabethan experience. The characters of the piece (particuarly the men) are obsessed with *expression*, rather than actual experience, and that includes the experience of love that the lords forswear in florid language, and then embrace in florid language.

THE CRITICS' CORNER

"Here is a fashionable play; now, by three hundred years, out of fashion. (Harley Granville-Barker.)

"(There is) a delicate raillery by Shakespeare himself at his own chosen manner." (Walter Pater)

LINES TO LISTEN FOR:

Navarre shall be the wonder of the
world;
Our court shall be a little academe,
Still and contemplative in living art.
(I, i)

If love make me forsworn,
how shall I swear to love?
(IV, ii)

Well, I do nothing in the world but
lie, and lie in my throat [i.e.,
"through my teeth"]. By heaven, I
do love, and it hath taught me to
rhyme and to be mallicholy [melan-
choly]. IV, iii

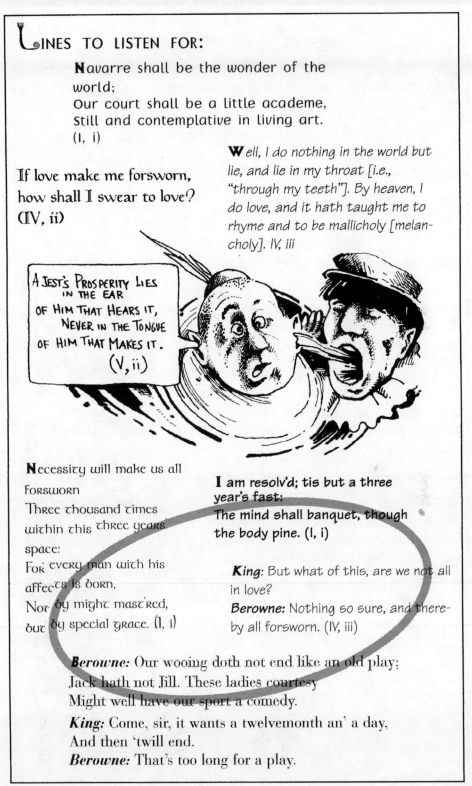

A JEST'S PROSPERITY LIES
IN THE EAR
OF HIM THAT HEARS IT,
NEVER IN THE TONGUE
OF HIM THAT MAKES IT.
(V, ii)

Necessity will make us all
forsworn
Three thousand times
within this three years'
space:
For every man with his
affects is born,
Not by might mast'red,
but by special grace. (I, i)

I am resolv'd; 'tis but a three
year's fast:
The mind shall banquet, though
the body pine. (I, i)

King: But what of this, are we not all
in love?
Berowne: Nothing so sure, and thereby all forsworn. (IV, iii)

Berowne: Our wooing doth not end like an old play;
Jack hath not Jill. These ladies courtesy
Might well have our sport a comedy.

King: Come, sir, it wants a twelvemonth an' a day,
And then 'twill end.
Berowne: That's too long for a play.

SOME COOL THINGS ABOUT LOVE'S LABOR'S LOST

5: The play appears to have been performed before Queen Elizabeth herself during the Christmas season of 1597.

4: There is no known direct source for the plot.

3: As Costard reveals in V, ii, the wench Jaquenetta is pregnant by Armado by the time the play reaches its conclusion. The verbose foreigner blusters about taking Costard's life for this revelation, but no blood is shed.

2: The appearance of the messenger in act V almost immediately follows the news of Jaquenetta's pregnancy. The real world is intruding on the comedy in uncomfortable and unforeseen ways.

I: Costard's extravagant use of the word **"honorificabilitudinitatibus"** (V, i) has given actors headaches for centuries. It's Latin for "the condition of being loaded down with honors," but the point, here as elsewhere, seems to be to emphasize the distancing nature of words.

WHERE LIES THE SCENE?
Verona.

WHAT HAPPENS?

Street fight! The Prince has had enough of the brawling between the **Montagues** and the **Capulets**. He issues an order under which any further public melee will result in death to the participants. **Romeo**, a Montague, declares himself to be in love with a young lady by the name of Rosaline. His companion **Benvolio** convinces him to attend a masked ball being thrown by the Capulets. Benvolio hopes to convince his friend that there are fairer women than **Rosaline** in the world. Benvolio acheives his objective; at the ball, Romeo meets and falls hopelessly for **Juliet,** a young woman of the Capulet family. Juliet, for her part, is similarly struck by the unknown young man, but is startled to learn his true identity. At the party, Juliet's kinsman **Tybalt** discovers Romeo's presence, but is dissuaded from making a scene by old Capulet. Romeo secretly visits Juliet. The two exchange vows of love and promise to be married the next day. Juliet, having informed the **Nurse** of her plans, sends her to Romeo the next day to finalize the details of the secret wedding. The two are married in Friar Laurence's cell. No sooner is he married than Romeo finds his two friends, **Mercutio** and **Benvolio**, involved in a tense discussion with the fiery Tybalt, who is seeking out Romeo. Tybalt tries in vain to start a fight, but Romeo, who realizes that the short-tempered Capulet is now his kinsman, will have none of it. Mercutio, however, is more than up to the task of initiating a quarrel, and in the ensuing fight he is slain. Romeo reacts in outrage at the death of his friend, and kills Tybalt. A crowd gathers as Romeo runs from the scene. · The Prince banishes Tybalt's killer. Romeo is shattered by recent events, but is heartened by a message from the equally distraught Juliet urging that he see her secretly that night. They spend the night together in her chamber; in the morning, he leaves her and escapes to Mantua. The Capulets, ignorant of their daughter's recent marriage, inform her that she is to be married to **Paris**, a relative of the Prince's. They are thunderstruck at her refusal. The Friar concocts an elaborate scheme under which Juliet is to appear to agree to the upcoming marriage; before the ceremony takes place, however, she will take a potion that will render her seemingly dead. According to the plan, Juliet will be carried to the Capulets' ancestral burial vault, where Romeo, who will be informed by the Friar of everything, will arrive when she awakens and spirit her away to Mantua. Juliet agrees to the plan. Fate is not with the lovers, however; the Friar's message to Romeo does not arrive, and he learns from someone else of his wife's "death" and believes her to have truly passed on. He buys poison, sets out for Verona, and arrives at Juliet's tomb — after having killed Paris, whom he encountered there. By his wife's side, Romeo takes the poison and dies. Awakening too late, Juliet sees her dead husband's body and, distraught, takes his dagger. She, too, dies by her own hand.

KEEP AN EAR OUT FOR ONGOING REFERENCES TO . . . Light, darkness, sudden explosions and flashes, stars, fate.

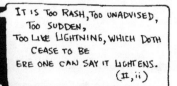

WHAT'S IT ALL ABOUT?

Romeo and Juliet is about love, of course, but it is about a particular kind of love: love that extinguishes itself. This story is fixated on the ideas of opposites, contradictions, and opposing pairs, and the focus throughout is on things that consume each other in a flash. This tragedy has less to do with the results of the choices the principals make than it does with the preordained failure of youthful passion — the passion of both awakening physical love and the sudden violence of a street quarrel.

We know that the lovers will die by the sixth line of this play. Romeo and Juliet relies heavily on notions of fate, destiny, and accident. The secret romance, the playful sexual banter of Mercutio, the long-standing feud, the delayed message from the Friar — all these seem at times to be part of a comedy gone terribly wrong, thanks to the dark influence of fate.

THE CRITICS' CORNER

"Romeo and Juliet is a picture of love and its pitiable fate, in a world whose atmosphere is too sharp for this the tenderest blossom of human life." (August Schlegel)

"This play presents a beautiful coup-d'oeil of the progress of human life. In thought it occupies years, and embraces the circle of the affections from childhood to old age." (William Hazlitt)

"Here (in Juliet) is a life cut short in its brightness; and it is a cruel business, this slaughter of a child betrayed." (Harley Granville-Barker)

LINES TO LISTEN FOR

Two households, both alike in dignity,
In fair Verona, where we lay our scene. (I, Prologue)

What's in a name?
That which we call a rose
By any other name would
smell as sweet. (II, ii)

These violent delights
have violent ends,
And in their triumph die;
like fire and powder
Which as they kiss consume.
(II, vi)

All things that we ordained festival
Turn from their office to black
funeral. (IV, v)

O, I am fortune's fool! (III, i)

More light and light,
more dark and dark our
woes! (III, v)

Thank
me no thankings, nor
proud me no prouds,
But fettle your fine joints 'gainst
Thursday next,
To go with Paris to Saint Peter's
Church,
Or I will drag thee on a hurdle
thither! (III, v)

The
sun, for
sorrow, will
not show
his head,
(V, iii)

Some Cool Things About Romeo and Juliet

5: The play's most direct source is a 1562 poem by Arthur Brooke, which was in turn based on a popular Italian story.

4: After Tybalt exits in act I, scene v, the two lovers recite an on-the-spot sonnet together. (A sonnet from the Chorus opens the play.)

3: The much-misunderstood line "Wherefore art thou Romeo?" (act II, scene ii) means "Why are you Romeo?" not "Where are you, Romeo?"

2: In a passage often cut in modern stage productions, the Friar, after announcing his intention to "be brief," recounts the entire plot of the story at some length (act V, scene ii).

1: The popular modern musical *West Side Story* is an adaptation of *Romeo and Juliet*, as is Gounod's 1867 opera *Romèo et Juliette*.

WHY NOT?

WHERE LIES THE SCENE?

England in the late fourteenth century

WHAT HAPPENS?

King Richard II, from Winsor castle, botching an attempt to mediate a dispute between **Henry Bolingbroke** and **the Duke of Norfolk**, exiles both men. When death claims Richard's uncle (and Bolingbroke's father) **John of Gaunt**, the king unwisely appropriates the dead man's wealth.

While King Richard is in Ireland, Bolingbroke invades England and claims his property. A number of noblemen, unhappy with Richard's rule, support his cause. Upon the king's arrival in Wales, he finds himself militarily and politically isolated. Richard withdraws to Flint Castle. Later, he yields to Bolingbroke, who escorts him to London.

Bolingbroke maneuvers his way to the crown. Richard is sent to the Tower of London, then to Pomfret Castle. The former Bolingbroke — now known as Henry IV — pardons a conspirator, the **Duke of Aumerle**, who had plotted against him.

The new king's exasperated complaint ("Have I no friend will rid me of this living fear?") leads to Richard's murder by Sir Pierce Exton, whom Henry subsequently banishes. The awesome consequences of Bolingbroke's ascent over Richard II, however, will haunt the new king for the rest of his life — and England for many years.

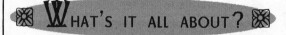 WHAT'S IT ALL ABOUT?

With *Richard II,* Shakespeare begins the second — and by far the stronger — of his two four-play cycles dealing with English history. The better to confuse generations of English students, he chose in the second series of plays to focus on an *earlier* set of events than those depicted in the previous *Henry VI — Richard III* cycle.

Richard is a complex, intellectually rigorous figure, but despite his keen perception and his amazing gift for language, he is a man fundamentally deceived by externals. More to the point, he is a poor politician and a poor leader.

Bolingbroke, on the other hand, the king's successor, may be cold and calculating, but he is neverthless a decisive man who does not indulge in Richard's habitual self-pity. Bolingbroke is certainly brave; he is capable of making sound decisions during trying times; and he is a far better judge of men than Richard.

One man, for all his faults, is the anointed King of England. The other, a realist who is more fit to wear the crown, replaces him. What consequences will this carry for the state?

Keep an ear out for ongoing references to...

Ceremony, emblems of royalty, gardens and orchards, trees and branches, brilliance, sunlight, kingship.

❧ 𝕿HE CRITICS' CORNER ❧

"Richard is not meant to be a debauchee; but we see in him that sophistry which is common to man, by which we can deceive our own hearts, and at one and the same time apologize for, and yet commit, the error." (Samuel Taylor Coleridge)

"Life is to Richard a show, a succession of images; and to put himself into accord with the aesthetic requirements of his position is Richard's first necessity." (Edward Dowden)

... THROW AWAY RESPECT, TRADITION, FORM, AND CEREMONIOUS DUTY, FOR YOU HAVE BUT MISTOOK ME ALL THIS WHILE. I LIVE WITH BREAD LIKE YOU, FEEL WANT, TASTE GRIEF, NEED FRIENDS: SUBJECTED THUS, HOW CAN YOU SAY TO ME I AM A KING? (III, ii)

LINES TO LISTEN FOR

God is the quarrel; for God's substitute,
His deputy anointed in his sight,
Hath caus'd his [Woodstock's] death; the
which if wrongfully,
Let heaven revenge; for I may never lift
An angry arm against his minister. (I, ii)

O. call back yesterday, bid time return! (III, ii)

... think our former state a happy dream;
From which awaked, the truth of what we are
Shows us but this. (V, i)

... within the hollow crown
That rounds the mortal temples of a king
Keeps Death his court.
(III, ii)

With mine own tears I wash away my balm,
With mine own hands I give away my crown,
With mine own tongue deny my sacred state,
With mine own breath release all duteous oaths;
All pomp and majesty I do forswear. (IV, i)

... our sea-wall'd garden, the whole land
Is full of weeds, her fairest flowers chok'd up,
Her fruit-trees all unprun'd, her hedges ruin'd,
Her knots disordered, and her wholesome herbs
Swarming with caterpillars ... (III, iv)

What must the King do now? Must he submit?
The King shall do it. Must he be depos'd?
The King shall be contented. Must he lose
The name of king? A God's name, let it go!
(III, iii)

IT'S ALL THE FAULT OF THEATRE!

Some cool things about Richard II

5: The Earl of Essex's supporters arranged for a performance of the play to be given at Shakespeare's Globe Theatre on February 7, 1601, the day before Essex's rebellion against Queen Elizabeth. The rebellion failed, and Essex was executed.

4: One of Shakespeare's pet peeves — the influence of hypocritical flatterers — shows up in John of Gaunt's warning to the King in act II, scene i. The playwright's loathing of people who offer false praise will eventually take the form of something akin to an obsession; later in his career, he will devote an entire play (*Timon of Athens*) to the subject.

3: Not one line of prose appears in **Richard II**; the play consists entirely of verse.

2: King Richard's agonized recounting of the emblems of royal status (act IV, scene i) contrast sharply with King Henry V's question in *Henry V*: ". . . what have kings, that privates have not too,/ Save ceremony, save general ceremony?" (act IV, scene i).

1: Richard is the first in a long line of Shakespeare's protagonists who just happens to speak superb poetry.

Where lies the scene?
Ancient Athens

What happens?

Old Egeus orders his daughter Hermia to wed Demetrius; she refuses, because she is in love with Lysander. Although the Duke of Athens sympathizes with Hermia's situation, he informs her that the law provides her with only three options: obey her father, join a convent, or forfeit her life. Lysander and Hermia plan to elope; they share their plan with Hermia's friend Helena. Later, Helena passes the news of the impending elopement along to Demetrius, in the hope of reawakening his love for her. It doesn't work. Meanwhile, in the realm of the fairies, King Oberon has been sharing harsh words with Queen Titania; he makes his aide, Puck, find a flower whose juice will make his Queen fall in love with the first person (or animal) she encounters after she wakes. The king sees Demetrius — pursuing Lysander and Hermia — and the unfortunate Helena, who has followed him into the forest, pleading for his affections. Taking pity on the unrequited love of Helena, the king instructs Puck to anoint the eyes of the young man she pines after. Puck, however, mistakenly puts the flower's juice on *Lysander's* eyes as he sleeps. When he awakes, the first person he sees is Helena, with whom he falls instantly in love. A group of craftsmen begins rehearsing a play they mean to perform before the Duke. The mischievous Puck places an ass's head upon the "player" who talks the most (and says the least), the weaver named Bottom. Bottom's friends flee in terror. Titania, who is nearby, wakes up, and, under the influence of the love juice, falls rapturously in love with Bottom. Oberon, attempting to rectify Puck's error, sees to it that Demetrius falls under the love spell. Demetrius does in fact fall in love with the long-suffering Helena, just as planned, but because Lysander is still under the spell's power as well, a scene of amatory chaos ensues. Order is finally restored when Puck removes the charm from the eyes of the sleeping Lysander. Oberon discovers Titania tending to her beloved, the ass-headed Bottom. The fairy king removes his spell and restores his queen to her senses;

Keep an ear out for ongoing references to . . . Madness, foolishness, imagination, animals, flora, weather, dreams.

Bottom is returned to his normal form. The Duke and his future wife, Hippolyta, encounter the four young lovers in the forest. Theseus overrides Egeus's objections and arranges for a triple wedding. At the wedding feast the craftsmen perform their amateur tragedy, which is unintentionally hilarious. The lovers retire to bed.

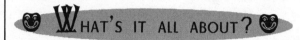

WHAT'S IT ALL ABOUT?

One of a few Shakespearean plays with no direct literary source, A Midsummer Night's Dream balances a feather-light series of romantic entanglements with brief but profound meditations on the illogical appeals of love, dreams, and the very poetry of the play itself. And what poetry! Like The Tempest — another play that appears to have been constructed from scratch by Shakespeare — A Midsummer Night's Dream pursues three sets of characters. Here, we follow the distracted lovers, the quarrelling supernatural king and queen, and the bungling amateur players who attempt to prepare their performance for the Duke. The three strands intersect perfectly, and together they acknowledge the importance of yielding, from time to time, to the unseen, unpredictable, and downright illogical demands of life. The world of rational discourse and artifice, the world of planned events, order, reason and sound, experienced, counsel, is the real dream world. The more profound reality is often to be discovered in accident, fantasy, and imagination.

"(T)he most insipid ridiculous play that ever I saw in my life." (Samuel Pepys.)

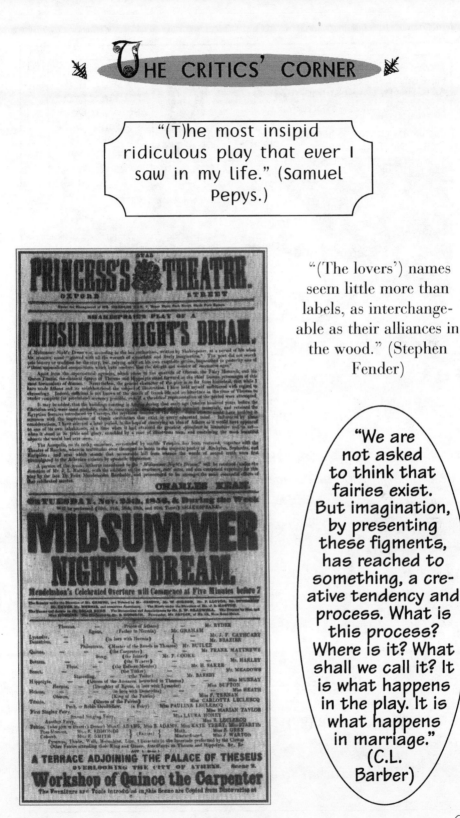

"(The lovers') names seem little more than labels, as interchangeable as their alliances in the wood." (Stephen Fender)

"We are not asked to think that fairies exist. But imagination, by presenting these figments, has reached to something, a creative tendency and process. What is this process? Where is it? What shall we call it? It is what happens in the play. It is what happens in marriage." (C.L. Barber)

LINES TO LISTEN FOR

The course of true love never did run smooth. (I, i)

The lunatic, the lover, and the poet
Are of imagination all compact [made up]. (V, i)

Things base and vile, holding no quantity,
Love can transpose to form and dignity. (I, i)

Thus die I, thus, thus, thus!
   [Stabs himself]
   Now am I dead,
   Now am I fled,
   My soul is in the sky.
   Tongue, lose thy light,
Moon, take thy flight, [Exit
   Moonshine]
Now die, die, die, die, die. (V, i)

. . . as imagination bodies forth
The forms of things unknown,
the poet's pen
Turns them to shapes. (V, i)

Lord, what fools these mortals be! (III, ii)

Some cool things about
A Midsummer Night's Dream

5: The rustics' performance of **Pyramus and Thisbe** serves two critical purposes: It reinforces the twin themes of illusion and reality, and it serves notice of the defeat of Death, who comes off looking more than a little ridiculous.

4: Hermia was played by a short boy in Shakespeare's troupe; Helena by a taller boy. (Note the size-related namecalling in act III, scene ii; Lysander dismisses Hermia as a "bead" and an "acorn.")

3: Some scholars believe that the stage direction for Bottom's entrance in the Folio text ("Enter Piramus with the Asse head") reflects the theatrical use of that text: the troupe apparently had one and only one ass's head.

2: The end of the play is a double benediction; Oberon blesses the lovers and assures them physically sound children (a tip of the hat to fertility, another triumph over death); Puck makes a final appeal to the audience's imaginative capacity before returning its members to the real world.

LOVERS, TO BED, 'TIS ALMOST FAIRY TIME. (V, i)

1: Many believe the play to have been commissioned especially for a wedding celebration.

WHERE LIES THE SCENE?

England and France during the reign of England's King John
(1199-1216.)

WHAT HAPPENS?

Upon the death of his brother **Richard I** (Richard the Lion-Hearted), **John**, supported by his mother **Elinor**, has assumed the throne under a dubious claim. **King Philip** of France insists, via an ambassador sent to the court of the English king, that the crown be surrendered to John's nephew, **Arthur**. The king refuses and prepares an invasion of France. One of the men at the head of his expedition is **Philip Faulconbridge** (the Bastard), the plain-spoken illegitimate son of Richard the Lion-Hearted. After an inconclusive battle at Angiers, King John agrees to a marriage that will render to Arthur certain disputed provinces in France. Disputes with the Pope lead to King John's excommunication and an end to the fragile, ill-conceived peace. The French are defeated at Angiers; young Arthur is captured by the King's forces, an event that sends his widowed mother Constance into her customary torrents of grief. The King orders **Hubert de**

Burgh to murder Arthur. **Lewis,** the Dauphin, makes plans to invade England and assume the crown. Young Arthur convinces Hubert de Burgh to spare his life, but the boy perishes from a fatal fall while trying to escape. There are defections from the king among important noblemen, who join forces with the recently-landed Dauphin. The Bastard remains loyal. In order to secure military aid, King John submits himself to the Church, surrendering his crown to the Pope's legate, then receiving it back again. In so doing, he fulfills a prophecy that he would give up his crown. A bloody but indecisive round of fighting follows; it ends when the defecting English noblemen learn that the Dauphin plans to execute them upon his victory. The noblemen return to the English party. King John dies, apparently as the result of being poisoned. The Pope's legate arranges a workable peace between the warring parties; John's son Henry assumes the throne. The Bastard proclaims that English unity can help the new king overcome any obstacle.

The world that the small-spirited, ethically challenged King John inhabits, like the ones Henry IV and Henry V will occupy, is complicated, corrupt, and fraught with difficult choices. The ones John makes are unlikely to endear him to an audience. Although this uneven, wordy play is one of the least frequently produced of Shakespeare's dramas, it is most noteworthy for the character of the courageous and loyal Bastard, Faulconbridge, who serves as a representative of virtuous, patriotic values lacking in the king. The howling widow Constance helps to reinforce the dark nature of John's usurpation of the throne.

THE CRITICS' CORNER:

"(Constance is the) wildest of Shakespeare's widows, this queen of all his wailing women, this wonderful and terrible poetess who is so amazingly accomplished in the dialectic of grief." (Mark Van Doren)

"Stylistically, King John is marked by tumid rhetoric. It is filled with violent action, but the action often serves as the occasion for debate or disputation, and consequently the play is very verbal." (Herschel Baker)

LINES TO LISTEN FOR:

Since kings break faith upon commodity,
Gain, be my lord, for I will worship thee! (II, i)

> **M**y name is Constance, I was Geffrey's wife,
> Young Arthur is my son, and he is lost.
> I am not mad, I would to heaven I were!
> For then 'tis like I should forget myself.
> O, if I could, what grief should I forget!
> Preach some philosophy to make me mad,
> And thou shalt be canoniz'd, Cardinal . . . (III, iii)

To gild refined gold, to paint the lily,
To throw a perfume on the violet . . .
Is wasteful and ridiculous excess. (IV, ii)

I am amaz'd methinks, and lose my way Among the thorns and dangers of this world. (IV, iii)

> *King John:* Death.
> *Hubert:* My lord?
> *King John:* A grave.
> *Hubert:* He shall not live.
> *King John:* Enough. (III, iii)

Away with me, all you whose souls abhor,
The uncleanly savours of a slaughter-house;
For I am stifled with this smell of sin. (IV, iii)

This England never did, nor never shall,
Lie at the proud foot of a conqueror
But when it first did help to wound itself. (V, vii)

WAR! WAR! NO PEACE! PEACE IS TO ME A WAR. (III, i)

8OME COOL THINGS ABOUT KING JOHN

> MAGNA CARTA ?
> SOMETHING ELSE TO SIGN.
> WHY DID I EVER WANT THIS JOB?

5: Although the historical King John is remembered primarily for signing (under compulsion) the Magna Carta treaty in 1215 guaranteeing feudal rights, no mention of that event appears in this play.

4: The scene between King John and Hubert in which the king orders Arthur's death (Act III, scene iii) is one that shows the dawning of Shakespeare's mature verse style. It displays a technical confidence and sense of rhythm that would resurface in, for instance, the terrified exchange after the offstage murder of Duncan in *Macbeth*.

3: The Bastard's famous speech on commodity (what we would call "expediency" or "opportunism") occurs at the end of act II, scene i. It's probably the play's most effective long speech.

2: Scholars are unsure about the date of the play's composition, and about its relationship to an old play called *The Troublesome Reign of King John*.

1: King John is part of neither the first tetralogy (*Henry VI, Parts One, Two, and Three*, and *Richard III*) nor the second (*Richard II, Henry IV, Parts One and Two*, and *Henry V*).

WHERE LIES THE SCENE?
Venice and Belmont.

WHAT HAPPENS?

Portia, a wealthy and beautiful young woman of Belmont, is courted by a number of suitors, among them **Bassanio**. He is short of cash, and he appeals to his friend **Antonio** (the title character) for help on this score during the courtship. Antonio agrees to lend his friend three thousand ducats for a period of three months, but in order to supply the funds, he himself must borrow a sum from a Jewish money-lender, **Shylock**. Shylock agrees to supply the loan with no interest — but only if Antonio agrees "in a merry sport" to a clause that allows Shylock to cut off a pound of Antonio's flesh in the event of a forfeiture. Antiono, who expects ships loaded with goods to arrive soon, agrees to the bond. Bassanio prepares to head for Belmont, planning to take with him his friend Gratiano and Shylock's former servant Launcelot Gobbo. Before he leaves, there is a party at which Shylock is in attendance. The money-lender's daughter Jessica sees her in father's absence the opportunity to elope with Lorenzo, a friend of Bassanio's. She steals money from her father and runs away. The event breaks Shylock's heart. Portia, in Belmont, subjects her suitors to a test imposed by a clause in her father's will. They must choose from three caskets, one lead, one silver, and one gold. Only the man who chooses the right casket will win Portia's hand. The first suitor selects the golden casket, and finds in it only a mocking message. The second suitor picks the silver casket, and is also rebuked by the message he finds inside. Bassanio, whom Portia immediately favors, arrives in Belmont. With the help of some prompting, he selects the lead casket. Within it, he finds her portrait. All the news that follows seems to be remarkably good: Gratiano and Nerissa, Portia's serving-maid, are in love, as are Jessica and Lorenzo. But word comes from Venice that cuts the merry-making short: Antonio's ships have met with misfortune, and he has forfeited his bond to Shylock. There is a hasty marriage between Bassanio and Portia, after which Portia quickly sends (the now-wealthy) Bassanio back to Venice to aid his friend. · Antonio's case goes before a court of justice; a young "doctor of Rome" appears to help resolve it. This young "man" is in reality Portia in disguise, accompanied by Nerissa, who is pretending to be a clerk. After a memorable discourse on mercy, Portia suggests that Shylock accept three times the amount of money in question. Shylock refuses all offers to resolve the debt, focusing on the letter of the law and citing the forfeiture of the bond. He demands his pound of flesh. To the astonishment of the assembly, the young doctor of the law pronounces in Shylock's favor — but then points out that the letter of the bond entitles him only to flesh, and not to blood. In the end, the judgment goes against Shylock. He is penalized severely (for plotting against the life of a Venetian citizen) and ordered to convert to Christianity. Back in Belmont, the true identities of the Portia and Nerissa are revealed, thanks to a conceit involving rings granted as payment in Verona for the services of the young doctor of law and "his" clerk. We learn that three of Antonio's ships have come in. For most of the characters — but not for Shylock — mercy has carried the day.

Keep an ear out for ongoing references to . . . Music, animals (especially dogs and wolves), mercy, money.

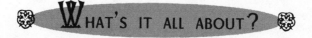

Shylock has a tendency to overshadow the other figures who populate the world of *The Merchant of Venice*. Dark questions of anti-Semitism relating to Shakespeare's immortal villain not only pass over the cultural context in which the play was written, but also tend to ignore Shakespeare's approach to egotism in his characters. Shylock's inhumanity is most notable not because he is Jewish, but because he represents the polar opposite of the forgiveness and mercy embodied by Portia. The truth is, Shakespeare's plays often feature disruptive, self-absorbed people who do not fit harmoniously into the social order. In *Twelfth Night*, Malvolio is imprisoned for a time and remains a bitter, selfish man after his release. Falstaff, from the *Henry IV* plays, is disowned by the king; we learn in *Henry V* that he dies a broken man. (Shakespeare also makes a point of killing off most of Prince Hal's youthful companions.) Shakespeare treats Shylock harshly, but that treatment is not without precedent.

WHAT'S YOU EXPECT: LIPOSUCTION?

THE CRITICS' CORNER

"There is morality in The Merchant of Venice, though it is not of the formulable kind; nor is it a morality on the level of the deepest insights expressed in the play." (John Middleton Murry)

"(Shylock is) a man thrust into a world bound not to endure him." (Mark Van Doren)"

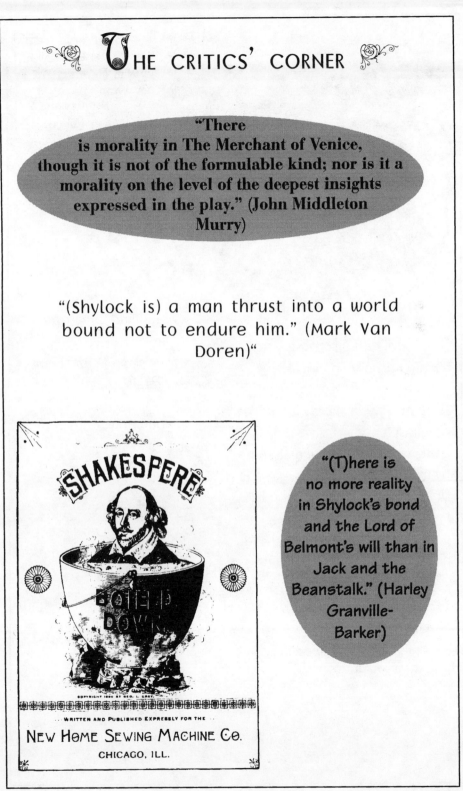

SHAKESPERE

BOILED DOWN

COPYRIGHT 1890 BY GEO. L. GRAY.

... WRITTEN AND PUBLISHED EXPRESSLY FOR THE ...

NEW HOME SEWING MACHINE CO.

CHICAGO, ILL.

"(T)here is no more reality in Shylock's bond and the Lord of Belmont's will than in Jack and the Beanstalk." (Harley Granville-Barker)

IF YOU PRICK US, DO WE NOT BLEED? IF YOU TICKLE US, DO WE NOT LAUGH? IF YOU POISON US, DO WE NOT DIE? AND IF YOU WRONG US, SHALL WE NOT REVENGE? (III, i)

LINES TO LISTEN FOR

The Devil can cite Scripture for his purpose. (I, iii)

The quality of mercy is not strain'd;
It droppeth as the gentle rain from heaven
Upon the place beneath. It is twice bless'd:
It blesseth him that gives and him that takes. (IV, i)

How far that little candle throws his beam!
So shines a good deed in a naughty world. (V, i)

But love is blind, and lovers cannot see
The petty follies that themselves commit. (II, vi)

I pray you tarry; pause a day or two
Before you hazard; for in choosing wrong
I lose your company.
Therefore forbear awhile.
There's something tells me (but it is not love)
I would not lose you, and you know yourself
Hate counsels not in such a quality [way]. (III, ii)

The man that hath no music in himself,
Nor is not mov'd with concord of sweet sounds,
Is fit for treasons, stratagems, and spoils. (V, i)

5: Romantic, imagination-laced Belmont serves as a contrast to commercial, hard-nosed Venice.

4: Shakespeare almost certainly did *not* construct his portrait of Shylock based on first-hand experiences with Jews, as they had been banished from England since the days of Edward I. (A Jewish Portugese physician named Roderigo Lopez was, however, tried and put to death for his role in a supposed plot against the life of Queen Elizabeth in 1594, three years before this play was probably completed.)

I'M SORRY. JEWS I DIDN'T KNOW.

3: The deep friendship between Antonio and Bassanio — a friendship whose changing nature has apparently led Antonio into a depression as the play begins — has given rise to speculations of homosexual love on Antonio's part, but this theme is never addressed directly in the text.

2: The play is composed of stories arising from several sources, the most notable of which is Ser Giovanni Fiorentino's *Il Pecorone* (composed circa 1378), which features a wooing scene, a usurous Jew, and new bride who disguises herself as a lawyer.

1: Confusion about the names of the friends of Antonio and Bassanio crops up at various points. There's one named Salanio, one named Salerio, and, just for good measure, one named Salarino, which appears to have been another name for Salerio that Shakespeare forgot to revise throughout the manuscript. (He had a way of spacing out on such matters.) Most editors combine the Salarino and Salerio lines to yield one acting part. You decide what to call him.

WHERE LIES THE SCENE?

England in the early fifteenth century.

WHAT HAPPENS?

PART ONE:

King Henry IV plans to make a pilgrimage to the Holy Land in penance for his part in the death of Richard II, but an uprising on the part of the northern barons forces him to change his plans. Henry Percy and his son (the valiant hothead nicknamed Hotspur), as well as the Welsh warrior Owen Glendower, present the king with a serious and increasingly bloody crisis. Apparently of little aid in this dire situation is King Henry's son Prince Hal, who spends most of his time in the company of a fat old knight by the name of John Falstaff. Thanks to his association with Falstaff, the Prince of Wales is thought by many, including his father, to be pursuing the life of a wastrel. The comparison between the Prince of Wales and Henry Percy's son Hotspur is drawn, and it is not flattering to the prince. He himself knows his true destiny, however. · After taking part in a plot involving a double robbery that proves Falstaff to be a coward, a liar, and an all-around scoundrel, Prince Hal proves his valor during the battle of Shrewsbury by killing Hotspur.

PART TWO:

The Earl of Northumberland learns, after a number of inaccurate reports about the battle of Shrewsbury, that his son has been killed in battle, and that the forces of Prince John are marching against him. He prepares to continue the rebellion, which is supported by Archbishop Scroop. The reprobate Falstaff continues to pursue his inimitable double-dealing lifestyle. Prince Hal tracks him down and engages in a bit of fun, disguising himself as a waiter while Falstaff says rude things about him, then revealing himself and challenging the old knight. He abruptly concludes the lighthearted interview to attend to more important duties. The king, gravely ill, longs for a conclusion to the wars, and restates his wish to travel to the Holy Land to show repentance for the death of Richard II. Falstaff renders service as a (thoroughly corrupt) military recruiter. News of the Earl of Northumberland's decision to desert the rebellion and wait in Scotland reaches the Archbishop. An envoy from Prince John invites the Archbishop and the rebel leaders Mowbray and Hastings to a peace conference to discuss their grievances; they agree to attend, and the talks appear to lead to a peaceful compromise. Once the rebellious troops are dispersed, the prince arrests the leaders, charging them with high treason, and orders their execution. Falstaff manages to evade anything vaguely resembling hazardous military duty, and pursues his customary dishonest dealings. After an uneasy reconciliation, King Henry opens his heart to his son, acknowledges his wrongdoings, and urges foreign campaigns as a means of distracting domestic rivals. The king dies. Prince Hal becomes King Henry V and, although the fat knight expects a different outcome, the new monarch repudiates Falstaff. The young man once thought too shallow to wield power effectively is prepared to lead his nation.

WHAT'S IT ALL ABOUT?

The two **Henry IV** plays explore serious questions of guilt, honor, maturity, the consequences of pragmatism, and the most sobering issues of atonement — and they somehow manage to be hilarious at the same time. With great difficulty, the king consolidates his position — and as he does so, we, like Hal, enjoy ourselves perhaps a little too much while we're in the company of the fat braggart knight John Falstaff. As many critics have noted, Falstaff is one of several characters introduced in these plays who resolutely refuses to mature. (The valiant, unforgettable Hotspur is another.) The brilliant, self-serving fat man strives manfully to present vice as virtue; he seems to exemplify the idea that a man who can make people laugh can get away with just about anything. For a while. In the end, Hal must reject him, and so must the audience. It takes an effort. When his friend Falstaff pleads, in Part One, that he not be banished from the prince's company in the end, Hal's response is both part of the gag of the moment — and a chillingly direct reflection of his true intentions. "Banish plump Jack, and banish all the world!" the fat old man laughs. "I do, I will," replies the future monarch. Despite appearances, Hal thinks in the long term.

THE CRITICS' CORNER

"(N)o man is more dangerous than he that with a will to corrupt, hath the power to please; and that neither wit nor honesty ought to think themselves safe with such a companion when they see Henry seduced by Falstaff."
(Samuel Johnson)

Prince Hal's humor is seasoned with sportsmanlike cruelty and the insolence of conscious mastery and contempt to the point of occasionally making one shudder." (George Bernard Shaw)

"Although the subplot concerning Falstaff is highly diverting, the major concern is hal's decision to embrace his role as hotspur's rival, abandoning the life of a barfly for that of a military leader." (Charles Boyce)

ꞏ⧫ LINES TO LISTEN FOR ⧫ꞏ

I prithee, sweet wag, shall there be gallows standing in England when thou art king? (I, ii)

I know you all, and will awhile uphold
The unyok'd humor of your idleness. (Part One, I, ii)

Glendower: I can call spirits from the vasty deep.
Hotspur: Why, so can I, or so can any man —
But will they come when you do call for them? (Part One, III, i)

If all the year were playing holidays,
To sport would be as tedious as to work.
But when they seldom come, they wish'd for come,
And nothing pleaseth but rare accidents. (Part One, I, ii)

Let the end try the man. (Part Two, II, ii) Thus we play the fools with the time, and the spirits of the wise sit in the clouds and mock us. (Part Two, II, ii)

The better part of valor is discretion. (Part One, V, iv)

LINES TO LISTEN FOR CON'T

O thou fond [foolish] Many! with what loud applause Didst thou beat heaven with blessing Bolingbroke Before he was what thou wouldst have him be! And being now trimm'd in thine own desires, Thou (beastly feeder) art so full of him That thou provok'st thyself to cast him up. (Part Two, I, iii)

Then you perceive the body of our kingdom, How foul it is; what rank diseases grow, And with what danger, near the heart of it. (Part One, III, i)

Uneasy lies the head that wears a crown. (Part Two, III. i)

What is honor? A word. What is that word honor? Air. A trim reckoning! Who hath it? Him that died a Wednesday. (Part One, V, i)

I can get no remedy against this consumption of the purse; borrowing only lingers and lingers it out, but the disease is incurable. (Part Two, I, ii)

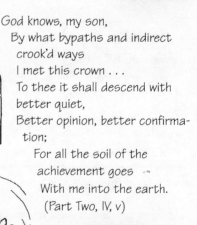

THUS WE PLAY THE FOOLS WITH TIME, AND THE SPIRITS OF THE WISE SIT IN THE CLOUDS AND MOCK US. (PART TWO, II, ii)

God knows, my son, By what bypaths and indirect crook'd ways I met this crown . . . To thee it shall descend with better quiet, Better opinion, better confirmation; For all the soil of the achievement goes With me into the earth. (Part Two, IV, v)

I know thee not, old man. Fall to thy prayers. (Part Two, V, v)

Some cool things about
Henry IV

6: Falstaff and Hotspur serve as extreme (and opposite) examples from which Hal must learn, and also as men whose example he must transcend if he is to govern well as king.

5: The residents of the occasionally less-than-savory world that revolves around Falstaff boast some of Shakespeare's best character names: the prostitute Doll Tearsheet (hmmm...), the military recruits Feeble, Wart, and Shadow (they come off just as intimidating in person), and the malaprop-challenged hostess of the Boar's Head Tavern, Mistress Quickly.

4: The seemingly awkward prologue that opens Part Two ("Rumor, painted full of tongues,") serves, among other things, to remind the audience of the dead Hotspur's pivotal role in the story.

3: Hotspur makes another "offstage appearance" in act II, scene iii of Part 2, when Lady Percy holds her father the Earl of Northumberland responsible for not accompanying Hotspur on the field of battle.

2: Hal tells us early on in that he intends to reform himself in such a way as to maximize the effect on his observers. (See the speech at the end of act I, scene ii, in Part One.)

1: Textual clues in early printed editions of Part One indicate that Falstaff was originally named Oldcastle, in keeping with one of Shakespeare's dramatic sources that chronicled Prince Hal's doings. A power- ful descendant of Sir John Oldcastle may have had something to do with the name change.

WHERE LIES THE SCENE?
Messina

WHAT HAPPENS?

Don Pedro, Prince of Arragon, accompanied by **Benedick** and **Claudio**, pays a visit to **Leonato**, the duke of Messina. Leonato is the father of **Hero**, with whom Claudio falls in love, and the uncle of **Beatrice**. This intelligent young woman makes a habit of engaging in witty verbal assaults on Benedick — a man who prides himself in his status as a confirmed bachelor, and who responds in kind to Beatrice's teasing. Claudio and Hero arrange to marry; Beatrice and Benedick are the subjects of an intrigue designed to make them fall in love. Benedick hears the Prince and Claudio discussing how deeply Beatrice loves Benedick. Beatrice overhears a similar conversation relating to Benedick's feelings for her. The two are brought together. The evil Don John "the bastard", hoping to disrupt the marriage of Hero and Claudio, causes Claudio to doubt his intended's fidelity by means of an overheard discussion between Don John's follower Borachio and Hero's maid, dressed as Hero. The trick convinces not only Claudio, but the Prince himself. On the wedding day, Claudio rejects Hero and speaks scornfully of her in front of the assembly. The Prince supports Claudio's assertions. Hero faints. After the debacle, Leonato spreads the word that his daughter has died, although she has not. Benedick, acting on Beatrice's fury at Claudio, issues a challenge to the young man. The unlikely discovery of Borachio's trick is made through Dogberry, a constable who mangles his English. The deceit is exposed. Claudio repents to Leonato, and offers to do anything in recompense to him. Leonato informs him he must marry Hero's cousin. This "cousin" appears at the ceremony masked, and is revealed to be Hero herself. Beatrice and Benedick also agree to marry.

Keep an ear out for ongoing references to . . .

Sound, music, outdoor contests, dance and movement.

WHAT'S IT ALL ABOUT?

The battle of the sexes continues, as it always does. Although Beatrice and Benedick, from a technical point of view, are part of the subplot, they are the characters people usually remember when they think of this satisfying balancing act of a comedy. The witty "battle" between the supposedly reluctant lovers helps to take the edge off the play's dominant story: the grave miscalculation made by Claudio and Don Pedro about Hero. The accusation she faces is a dark thread that might, in another play (such as Othello), initiate a tragedy. In later works, such as Measure for Measure or All's Well That Ends Well, the darkness will be far more difficult to overcome. For now, however, the threatening clouds remain, but do not blot out some welcome, and transforming, rays of sunlight. Potentially catastrophic misunderstandings arise, and threaten even the male solidarity of the comrades in arms (that's quite a threat, to the Elizabethan way of thinking); the deceptions are revealed, and solidarity is restored. The clown Dogberry has "had losses" of an unknown kind, but somehow his struggles with the villains (if not those with the English language) result in success. Appropriately, the play concludes with a conscious decision to "think not on" the villain of the piece "till to-morrow," and to dance instead.

THE CRITICS' CORNER

"A shocking bad play." (George Bernard Shaw) "(Shakespeare's) most perfect comic masterpiece." (Algernon Charles Swinburne) "Don John is a malcontent pure and simple, a man who might say with the cold duke in Thurber's story, 'We all have faults, and mine is doing wickedness.'" (Anne Barton) "(Only) precariously does comedy arrive at its final celebration of joy, harmony and good fortune." (Levi Fox)

LINES TO LISTEN FOR

I would my horse had the speed of your tongue. (I, i)

Every one can master a grief but he that has it. (III,ii)

One woman is fair, yet I am well; another is wise, yet I am well; another virtuous, yet I am well; but till all graces be in one woman, one woman shall not come in my grace. (II, iii)

Don Pedro: . . . (T)o be merry best becomes you, for out a' question you were born in a merry hour.
Beatrice: No, sure, my lord, my mother cried, but then there was a star danc'd, and under that I was born.

(H)e (Benedick) hath a heart as sound as a bell and his tongue is the clapper, for what his heart thinks his tongue speaks. (III, ii)

. . . **T**here was never yet philosopher
That could endure the toothache patiently. (V, i)

I yield upon great persuasion, and partly to save your life, for I was told you were in a consumption. (V, iv)

(A) college of wit-crackers cannot flout me out of my humor. (V, iv)

Some cool things about Much Ado About Nothing

5: Hero's supposed death serves as this play's example of the comic form's triumph over mortality. Similar raspberries are blown in the direction of the Grim Reaper in, for example, **A Midsummer Night's Dream.**

4: Dogberry winds up in a tie with Mistress Quickly (of the **Henry IV** plays and **Henry V**) for the Abuse of the English Language trophy. Like the far more skilled verbal opponents Beatrice and Benedick, he uses language as a kind of self-protection.

3: Beatrice's startling command to Benedick after the two finally acknowledge their love for one another ("Kill Claudio") is one of the play's high points.

2: The two intersecting stories reflect lighter (Beatrice and Benedick) and graver (Hero and Claudio) treatments of the themes of eavesdropping and deception. Lightness carries the day.

1: Berlioz elevated the play's subplot to the main plot in his 1861 opera ***Bèatrice et Bènèdict.***

HENRY V

WHERE LIES THE SCENE?

Early fifteenth-century England

WHAT HAPPENS?

Following his late father's advice to pursue foreign initiatives, **the king** resolves to invade France and claim its crown as his own. **The Dauphin** responds contemptuously to the English king's claim for certain lands, forwarding a mocking gift of tennis balls. The king responds that the gesture will be one the French people will regret. The death of **Falstaff** is reported. The king uncovers a French-financed plot to murder him; he orders the conspirators, all of them English noblemen, executed. All of England unites under King Henry's cause. The French court makes ready for war. The Dauphin, remembering Henry's reputation as a prince, argues that the English enemy is "idly king'd." The English forces win an important battle at Harfleur. **Bardolph**, a friend of the king's from his youthful days, is hanged for robbing a church. The French send an envoy demanding ransom; the king refuses to abandon his campaign, and his increasingly weary army presses forward. Facing seemingly insurmountable odds, the English prepare for a battle with the French. The night before the battle, he walks in disguise among his men, then prays that God will not bring his cause to defeat as punishment for his father's treatment of Richard II. In the morning, the king refuses another request for ransom at Agincourt, and eloquently declares his faith in his cause. Amazingly, the smaller English forces carry the day. In what may be his most impressive victory of all, Henry woos and wins **Katherine**, daughter of the French king. The expedition concludes in triumph.

WHAT'S IT ALL ABOUT?

Although the mature king at the center of *Henry V* is a supremely charismatic figure — nothing less than the savior of the nation — he is wrapped in disturbing enigmas. The horrific language Henry uses to predict his army's slaughter and abuse of the residents of Harfleur (act III, scene iii) is not what an audience may expect to hear from a supposedly "sympathetic" king. Yet this play, and the three that have preceded it, have focused time and time again on the many difficulties of the craft of leadership, and on the odd blend of opportunism and honor required to be both a good man and a good king. It may only be after we have seen or read this scene several times that we realize that Henry's terrifying speech, like any number of other potentially distancing moments in the play, perfectly serves the king's — and the nation's — long-term interests. By *talking* so eloquently about the slaughter that will follow if the citizens do not relent, Henry hopes not to have to *enact* that slaughter by ordering his men into battle. The town yields immediately to the king. · Similarly difficult moments — Henry's reaction to the death of his old friend Bardolph (act III, scene vi), or his order to murder the French prisoners of war (the final lines of act IV, scene vi) — make it clear that this king is a complex pragmatist who is willing to use unconventional means to fulfill his own high standards. Henry is not a paper king in love with the trappings of his own royalty, but an active, engaged participant in the chaotic world in which he knows that he lives. He is, in short, not Richard II, which is fortunate for England.

Keep an ear out for ongoing
references to . . .
Speed, thought, language and speech,
ceremony, kingship.

THE CRITICS' CORNER

"One can hardly forgive Shakespear quite for the worldly phase in which he tried to thrust such a Jingo as his Harry V down our throats." (George Bernard Shaw)

"How English he is — so practical, sportsmanlike, moral, and pious; so manly and stalwart, and yest free and easy; so self-assertive and yet modest and generous; so fierce against his enemies, and yet merciful towards women and the weak; so serious, and yet simple and humorous; and so bluff and downright, and hearty and genuine, in the avowal of his love." (Elmer Edgar Stoll)

LINES TO LISTEN FOR:

O for a Muse of fire, that would ascend
The brightest heaven of invention . . . (Prologue)

King Henry: May I with right and conscience make this claim?
Canterbury: The sin upon my head, dread sovereign. (I, ii)

Things may be as they may. Men may sleep, and they may have their throats about them at that time; and some say knives have edges. It must be as it may. (II, i)

The mercy that was quick in us but late,
By your own counsel is suppress'd and kill'd. (II, ii)

Now I, to comfort him [Falstaff], bid him 'a should not think of God; I hop'd there was no need to trouble himself with any such thoughts yet. So 'a bade me lay more clothes on his feet. I put my hand into the bed and felt them, and they were as cold as any stone; then I felt to his knees, and so up'ard and up'ard, and all was as cold as any stone. (II, iv)

GENTLEMEN IN ENGLAND, NOW-A-BED, SHALL THINK THEMSELVES ACCURS'D THEY WERE NOT HERE; AND HOLD THEIR MANHOODS CHEAP WHILES ANY SPEAKS THAT FOUGHT WITH US UPON SAINT CRISPIN'S DAY.
(IV, iii)

Once more unto the breach, dear friends, once more;
Or close the wall up with our English dead. (III, i)

All things are ready, if our minds be so. (IV, iii)

Katherine: Is it possible dat I sould love de ennemie of France?
King Henry: No, it is not possible that you should love the enemy of France, Kate; but in loving me, you should love the friend of France; for I love France so well that I will not part with a village of it.

SOME COOL THINGS ABOUT HENRY V

5: Laurence Olivier's 1944 film version of the play omitted the king's reaction to the news of Bardolph's execution for stealing a church money-box. Kenneth Branagh's 1989 production made Henry's speech after Bardolph's hanging the emotional center-piece of the film.

4: Katherine's attempts to learn English (act III, scene iv) shows that Shakespeare could get laughs even when writing in another language.

3: Henry's shocking order to kill his prisoners of war, another detail frequently omitted in stage and film productions, is historically accurate.

2: The report of the death of Falstaff (act II, scene iii) mirrors the careful references to the dead Hotspur in **Henry IV, Part Two**. Quickly's speech about the fat old knight's passing is one of the most touching in any of the history plays.

1: The role of the Chorus is a rarity: an "expositional" part that actors would give their eye teeth to play.

HEY, I DIDN'T ORDER IT! I ONLY REPORTED IT!

JULIUS CAESER

WHERE LIES THE SCENE?

Rome, circa 44 B.C.

WHAT HAPPENS?

The Roman dictator **Julius Caesar** returns in triumph from a successful military campaign. **Cassius** and **Casca** are uneasy about Caesar's ambition; they plot a conspiracy against him and enlist the support of the noble and idealistic Brutus, who has his misgivings about the undertaking, but agrees to participate because of his concern for the future Roman republic. Caesar is slain in the Capitol, despite the warnings of a soothsayer. When he sees the trusted **Brutus** among the conspirators, he cries "Et tu, Brute?" ("And you, Brutus?") **Antony**, "well beloved of Caesar," pretends to accede to the wishes of the conspirators — but when the conspirators commit the mistake of giving him the chance to speak directly to the Roman people during Caesar's funeral, he incites the populace against the murderers by delivering a remarkable speech. Julius Caesar's nephew **Octavius** unites with Antony and **Lepidus**

in opposition to Brtus and Cassius. The complex relationship between Brutus and Cassius faces a series of awesome challenges. The two are finally defeated at the
Battle of Philippi, where they commit suicide. Brutus is
described as "the noblest Roman of them all" by Antony.

Keep
an ear out for ongoing references to . . .
Blood, animals, rituals, ceremony.

Julius Caesar may be one of the two best plays for a newcomer to Shakespeare. (The other nominee: *Romeo and Juliet*.) The language of the Roman drama is direct and accessible, and its action is clear. After an agony of indecision, Brutus acts. He longs for high purpose, rather than petty maneuvering, in the death of Caesar, the better to absolve himself — and Rome — of the guilt associated with the killing. But things fall apart. Caeser was haughty, self-absorbed, and devoted to a kind of leadership possibly incompatible with the interests of the nation. But where does Shakespeare stand on the morality of the decision to kill him before he can be crowned? It's hard to say, although the Bard obviously knows that the world of politics is a complicated one, and that idealistic expressions of principle often result in very different outcomes than those supposedly intended by the men who espouse them.

THE CRITICS' CORNER

"The killing of Julius Caesar in Shakespear, is either a Murder, or a Lawful Action; if the killing *Caesar* is a lawful action, then the killing of Brutus and Cassius is downright Murder; and the Poet has been guilty of polluting the Scene, with the Blood of the very Best and Last of the *Romans*." (John Dennis)

"Brutus is objecting to the *crowning* of Caesar; he is a man who attaches much importance to ceremony, even attempting to make a savage murder into a sort of ritual." (Frank Kermode)

Shall Rome stand under one man's awe? What, Rome? (II, i)

The fault, dear Brutus, is not in our stars But in our-selves that we are underlings. (I, ii)

Cowards die many times before their deaths; The valiant never taste of death but once. (II, ii)

There is a tide in the affairs of men, Which, taken at the flood, leads on to fortune; Omitted, all the voyage of their life Is bound in shallows and in miseries. (IV, iii)

Friends, Romans, countrymen, lend me your ears; I come to bury Caesar, not to praise him. The evil that men do lives after them, The good is oft interred with their bones. (III, ii)

. . . when I tell him he hates flatterers, He says he does, being then most flattered. (II, i)

BEWARE THE IDES OF MARCH. (I, ii)
THIS MESSAGE IS BROUGHT TO YOU BY THE PSYCHIC SOOTHSAYERS NETWORK.

We must take the current when it serves, Or lose our ven-tures. (IV, iii)

SOME COOL THINGS ABOUT JULIUS CAESAR

5: The main source for the play was Plutarch's history *Lives of the Noble Grecians and Romans,* translated by Sir Thomas North.

4: The use of rhetorical questions as weapons in the political arena is one of the most stirring and theatrically powerful recurring elements of the play.

3: Brutus is the first of Shakespeare's tragic protagonists whose inner conflicts are of greater interest than his outward actions. He wrestles with *himself* over the momentous decisions he must make, and has often been cited as a forerunner to Hamlet.

2: Caesar has a way of talking about himself in the third person ("Caesar shall go forth") that vividly illustrates the old man's very real pride and self-absorption.

HEY, IT SEEMED LIKE A GOOD IDEA AT THE TIME . . .

1: Brutus ultimately emerges as an unconvincing idealist, a high-minded politician guided by a commitment to honor . . . as he defines it.

W HERE LIES THE SCENE?
Illyria

W HAT HAPPENS?

A shipwreck separates the twins Viola and Sebastian. Viola ends up on the coast of Illyria; disguised as a boy, she is named the Duke of Orsino's page. While acting on behalf of the Duke in wooing Olivia, Viola finds that Olivia has fallen in love with the "boy" page. For her part, Viola must conceal her own increasing affections for the Duke. Olivia's maid Maria conspires with Olivia's uncle, Sir Toby Belch, and the foolish knight Sir Andrew Aguecheek, to send a mysterious love letter to the smug, insufferable steward Malvolio. They hope to fool Malvolio into believing that that letter is from Olivia. Malvolio slavishly follow's the letter's strange instructions, going so far as to wear crossed garters, a style Olivia loathes. Olivia concludes that he is disturbed, Malolio is later confined. Sir Toby provokes a duel between two unwilling combatants, Sir Andrew and the disguised Viola. Fortunately, the fight is broken up by Antonio, a sea captain who has come to Illyria. He believes Viola to ber her twin brother Sebastian, who has not, as Viola had supposed, drowned at sea. Later, Sir Andrew comes upon Sebastian and attempts to conclude the fight. Sebastian defeats him Olivia encounters Sebastian and believes him to be Orsino's page. She suggests marriage. Sebastian accepts. The Duke clears Viola of an accusation of theft made by the confused Antonio; Olivia, before the Duke, refers to the page as her husband, much to Orsino's anger. Awkward moments follow, but when Sebastian appears and discovers that his sister is alive, Viola's true identity is revealed. Orsino realizes that he is in love with Viola. Malvolio is set free, swearing revenge on those who tricked him. The play closes with a striking song about the passage of time and the inevitability of storms.

Keep an ear out for ongoing references to . . .
Celebration, festivity, music, excess.

MY THIS DOES SEEM TO HAPPEN ALOT.

THE DAILY GLOBE
TWINS SEPARATED IN BOATING TRAGEDY

So are you Cesario, are you Viola or are you me?

What's it all about?

The title refers to Epiphany, a holiday still known in Shakespeare's day as a time of festive renewal, an opportunity for temporary suspension of some of the guiding rules of the community. At this time of year, propriety had a way of being turned on its head. Such an illogical approach to life perturbs brow-wrinklers like Malvolio — and, for that matter, audience members who wonder about questions of plausibility. Shakespeare's advice to both types seems to be the same: Lighten up. All the same, a dark thread that prefigures the later romances appears in *Twelfth Night*. Olivia really has lost a brother, although her reaction to that event is excessive. The play's final song makes repeated reference to storms. In Viola's patient, open, pragmatic attitude to the perplexing obstacles she encounters in Ilyria, Shakespeare may be illuminating one strategy for responding to disconcerting and inevitable truths (like death).

The critics' corner

"(In *Twelfth Night* there is) a silvery tone of sadness, which makes it perhaps the loveliest of all Shakespeare's high comedies . . . Feste is an older, sadder, wiser man than Touchstone; and he has outworn his favor." (John Middleton Murry)

"Malvolio is potentially tragic, for he finds that past modes of behavior are no longer suitable, no longer meaningful in his present relationship with the world. His self-love is no longer adequate." (Sylvan Barnet)

LINES TO LISTEN FOR

If music be the food of love, play on,
Give me excess of it, that surfeiting [overindulging],
The appetite may sicken, and so die. (I, i)

Dost thou think, because thou art virtuous,
there shall be no more cakes and ale? (II, iii)

O, fellow, come — the song we had last night. (II, iv)

Some are born great, some achieve greatness, and some
have greatness thrust upon them. (II, 5)

When that I was and a little tiny boy,
With hey, ho, the wind and the rain,
A foolish thing was but a toy,
For the rain it raineth every day. (V, i)

5: Malvolio's brand of egotism, like Iago's in *Othello*, carries potentially serious consequences for the social order. Don't feel sorry for him; Olivia's steward deserves everything he gets.

4: Viola's declaration that "(Time) must untangle this, not I" (Act II, scene ii) complements Hamlet's hard-won realization that "If it be now, 'tis not to come; if it be not to come, it will be now; if it be not now, yet it will come . . .". (act V, scene ii).

3: Feste's impersonation of "Sir Topas," and his pronouncement that Malvolio is insane (act IV, scene ii), is rich in irony. From a certain point of veiw, Malvolio *is* insane. He refuses to allow the "insanity" of revelry into his life.

2: In the version of the play that survives, Sir Toby's language appears to have been cleaned up for the stage in response to anti-profanity statutes.

1: As many critics have pointed out, the play focuses on the merits of engaging in merrymaking or "indulgence" as a preliminary to gaining greater self-knowledge.

WORRIED ABOUT THIS 'INDULGENCE' BUSINESS? LET MY PAL, BILL, HAVE A GO:

THE ROAD OF EXCESS LEADS TO THE PALACE OF WISDOM.

AS YOU LIKE IT

WHERE LIES THE SCENE?

Duke Frederick's court and thereabouts; the forest of Arden

WHAT HAPPENS?

The rightful Duke has been living in exile with his loyal followers in the Forest of Arden, having been unjustly deprived of his dominions by his younger brother **Frederick**. As it happens, discord mars the relations of another pair of brothers: **Orlando**, the youngest son of **Sir Roland de Boys**, has been kept at home and deprived of the education he considers his right. While preparing to take part in a wrestling match with the fearsome champion **Charles**, Orlando is urged by **Celia**, the daughter of Duke Frederick, and **Rosalind**, the daughter of the exiled Duke, not to risk his life. Orlando wins the match, even though Charles had been encited by **Oliver** to do him grievous bodily harm. Frederick does not congratulate Orlando on his victory, but because of his past friendship with the exiled Duke, treats him rudely. Later, he banishes Rosalind. She resolves to disguise herself as a boy, and, accompanied by Celia and the clown Touchstone, she makes her way to the Forest of Arden. Oliver is in high wrath against his brother. Orlando, too, flees for the Forest of Arden, accompanied by **Adam**, his old servant. Rosalind and Celia dress as shepherds. Orlando draws his sword on the Duke's followers and demands something to eat, but the force is needless; he is persuaded to join the friendly band of hunters, who are happy with their pastoral lifestyle. (Happy, that is, with the exception of the cynical Jaques, who could be discontented with just about anything.) Duke Frederick, under the impression that the two young women have run away with Orlando, orders Oliver to deliver up his younger brother. Orlando, in love with Rosalind, hangs the poems he has composed for her on the trees of the forest. Later, disguised as a male shepherd, Rosalind pretends to rail against the very idea of love, and promises to cure Orlando of his love-sickness. All Orlando must do is woo "him" exactly as he would Rosalind. In her guise as the shepherd, Rosalind encounters the shepherdess **Phebe**, pined over by one **Silvius**. Phebe falls in love with the person she believes to be the young man of her dreams — Rosalind. In the meantime, the clown Touchstone has discovered the charms of a country wench named **Audrey**. Orlando, in order to be delivered from his bout of love-sickness, woos the "shepherd" as though "he" were Rosalind, which in fact he is. Later, Orlando saves his brother from an attack by a snake and a lion, and is detained from his appointed meeting with the "shepherd." Oliver offers the disguised Rosalind a bloody handkerchief as proof of the dangerous encounter. Oliver and Celia fall in love. Rosalind, still in disguise, promises the pining Orlando to cause Rosalind to appear by magic. She also fends off the affections of Phebe, making her promise to marry Silvius in the event she decides not to marry the "shepherd." · The next day, Rosalind appears dressed in her own clothing before theDuke and his followers. Four couples — Orlando and Rosalind, Oliver and Celia, Silvius and Phebe, and Touchstone and Audrey — prepare to be united in marriage. It is reported that Duke Frederick has undergone a religious conversion, and has seen to it that all confiscated lands be restored to their rightful owners.

In Shakespeare's "pastoral" comedy, extraordinary, transforming things happen in the forest of Arden. The forest is a magical place where heroes find their place in the social order, and those in error repent their transgressions. The play embraces and sends up ideals of pastoral romance, and the result is harmony. The cynical poseur Jacques mocks the vices of others, and is in turn mocked by both Rosalind and Touchstone for the self-assured, world-weary detachment he maintains so consciously. **As You Like It** presents a world in which clashing viewpoints on divisive matters eventually coexist. The reconciling tolerance and acceptance that Rosalind embodies ensures a newer, stabler kind of society, one that can laugh at itself.

Keep an ear out for ongoing references to...

Words, action, cynicism, melancholy, artifice, imagination, reality, balance.

THE CRITICS' CORNER

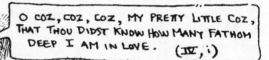

O COZ, COZ, COZ, MY PRETTY LITTLE COZ, THAT THOU DIDST KNOW HOW MANY FATHOM DEEP I AM IN LOVE. (IV, i)

LINES TO LISTEN FOR

And so from hour to hour we ripe and ripe,
And then from hour to hour we rot and rot,
And thereby hangs a tale. (II, vii)

I do desire we may be better strangers. (III, ii)

And so from hour to hour we ripe and ripe,
And then from hour to hour we rot and rot,
And thereby hangs a tale. (II, vii)

Blow, blow, thou winter
wind
Thou art not so unkind
As man's ingratitude. (II,
vii)

**All the world's a stage,
And all the men and women merely
players. They have their exits and their
entrances,
And one man in his time plays many
parts. (II, viii)**

The poor world is almost six thousand years old,
and in all this time there was not any man died in
his own person, videlicet, in a love cause . . . men
have died from time to time, and worms have
eaten them, but not for love. (IV, i)

**I knew when seven justices could not take up [resolve] a
quarrel, but when the parties were met themselves, one of
them thought but of an If, as, "If you said so, then I said
so": and they shook hands and swore brothers. Your If is
the only peacemaker; much virtue in If. (V, iv)**

How bitter a
thing it is to
look into hap-
piness
through
another
man's eyes!
(V, ii)

Some cool things about As You Like It

5: The famous "Seven Ages of Man" speech appears in act II, scene vii.

4: The play's source is Rosalynde: **Euphues Golden Legacie**, by Thomas Lodge, which was in turn based on a fourteenth-century poem called **The Tale of Gamelyn**.

3: Jacques' carefully maintained melancholy provides an interesting counterpart to Hamlet's "antic disposition."

2: When the disguised Rosalind offers to impersonate herself to "cure" Orlando, a dense fabric of gender confusion settles in. An Elizabethan audience would have seen a boy actor portraying a woman portraying a man portraying a woman!

1: Rosalind balances emotion and reason, the subjective and the objective, in a transforming way — and brings life to a new order.

SEVEN AGES? MOST MEN NEVER GET OUT OF ADOLESCENCE.

THE MERRY WIVES OF WINDSOR

WHERE LIES THE SCENE?

(Where else...?) Windsor.

WHAT HAPPENS?

Sir John Falstaff, short on cash, plans overtures to the virtuous wives of a pair of gentlemen, **Ford** and **Page**. (The two women have day-to-day control of their husbands' funds.) Disgruntled followers of the fat knight vow to issue warnings to Ford and Page. Mistress Page's daughter **Anne** is being sought by three suitors: a rich fool named **Slender**, a volatile, ill-spoken French doctor named **Caius**, and a high-spirited young gentleman named **Fenton**. Each suitor asks for the aid of **Mistress Quickly**, who makes as though she knows the inner workings of the young Anne's mind and shows a certain opportunism in her dealings with the men. Caius learns that Sir Hugh Evans has sent a letter in support of Slender; the Frenchman challenges the parson Evans to duel. The two wives compare love letters they have received from Falstaff. The letters are virtually identical, with only the names changed. They laugh at his folly and promise to make him pay for his overtures. Ford returns word that she is willing to meet with Falstaff. Having received reports of Falstaff's intentions toward their wives, the two husbands show markedly different reactions. Ford is intensely jealous; Page harbors no doubts as to his wife's fidelity. Ford disguises himself as one "Master Brook" and offers to pay Falstaff

for any help he can supply in proving Mistress Ford faithless —
and securing her for "Brook's" enjoyment as well. Caius and Evans,
both more interested in talking than fighting, settle their differ-
ences without a duel. Falstaff makes his way to Mistress Ford's;
when Mistress Page brings word that Ford's husband is on his way,
the knight is stuffed into a buck-basket, covered with filthy laundry, and sent out to be dumped in the water. Ford does in fact
appear; the women laugh at his jealous accusations. Falstaff
agrees to a second meeting with Mistress Ford. Her husband's
imminent arrival is again reported. Having had enough of dirty
laundry, the knight agrees to dress up as an old woman — one
that Ford recognizes and loathes. The furious husband beats the
daylights out of him, but never suspects the "woman's" true identity. The wives reveal their tormentings of Falstaff to their husbands, who agree to a final trick at his expense. Falstaff is
instructed to arrive in Windsor Forest wearing a buck's head; each
of the three suitors of Anne Page contrives to meet her there and
elope with her. Before he can enjoy the tryst he expects to share
with both wives, Falstaff is tormented by supposed "fairies" who
pinch him and set candles to him. Slender, instructed by Page to
run away from the scene with a fairy dressed in white, realizes
that his "bride" is a young boy. Caius, instructed by Mistress Page
to run away from the scene with a fairy dressed in green, finds
himself similarly disappointed. Fenton and Anne elope.

WHAT'S IT ALL ABOUT?

The principals of this play are not kings, queens, and dukes, but middle-class English folk who live near, but are not part of, the monarch's court. Despite the supposedly "real-world" atmosphere, the third and final play in which John Falstaff appears comes off as more forced than its predecessors **Henry IV, Part One** and **Henry IV, Part Two**. While **The Merry Wives of Windsor** is amusing enough, the fat knight never seems to emerge in three (ample) dimensions in quite the way he does in the earlier two plays. The plot puts Falstaff in the position of the outsider who poses a (never very real) danger to a harmonious social order; the play has a certain mechanical feel that doesn't approach the density and richness of either the history plays, or comedies such as **Much Ado** or **A Midsummer Night's Dream**. Few of Shakespeare's plays feel as much like a "vehicle" as this one does. The decision to make Falstaff the butt of a series of jokes, rather than an inspired improviser, seems to have taken a good deal of life out of the knight. Still, **The Merry Wives of Windsor** is a quick-moving, well constructed farce that has a pleasant enough way of making audiences laugh.

IT ISN'T EASY BEING A WOMAN.

THE CRITICS' CORNER

"In love, properly speaking, Falstaff could not be; but for other purposes he could pretend to be so, and at all events imagine that he was the object of love." (August Schlegel)

"That Queen Bess should have desired to see Falstaff making love proves her to have been, as she was, a gross-minded old baggage." (Hartley Coleridge)

"To picture the real Falstaff befooled like the Falstaff of the Merry Wives is like imagining Iago the gull of Roderigo . . " (A.C. Bradley)

> **What, have I scap'd love-letters in the holiday-time of my beauty, and am I now a subject of them? (II,i)**

Better three hours too soon than a minute too late. (II, ii)

Come, I cannot cog and say thou art this and that, like a many of these lisping hawthorn buds, that come like women in men's apparel . . . — I cannot; but I love thee, none but thee, and thou deserv'st it. (III, iii)

Good mother, do not marry me to yond fool! (III, iv)

We'll leave a proof, by that which we will *do*,
Wives may be merry, and yet honest too.
(IV, ii)

I will tell you, he beat me grievously in the shape of a woman. For in the shape of man, Master Brook, I fear not Goliah (Goliath) . . . (V, i)

Have I laid my brain in the sun and dried it, that it wants matter to prevent so gross o'erreaching as this? (V, v)

Keep an ear out for ongoing references to . . .
Games, springtime.

120

Some cool things about The Merry Wives of Windsor

5: Shakespeare, a writer unusually sensitive to smells throughout his career, makes a point of punishing Falstaff by stuffing him into a batch of dirty, reeking laundry.

4: The story appears to have no direct source.

3: The play within a play near the conclusion strongly recalls the rustics' performance in A Midsummer Night's Dream.

2: Falstaff's excited cry before what he believes will be a sexual tryst with Mistress Page — "Let the sky rain potatoes!" — reflects the Elizabethan belief that sweet potatoes were an aphrodisiac.

SOMETIMES YOU GOTTA GIVE 'EM WHAT THEY WANT.

1: Verdi's opera Falstaff is adapted from The Merry Wives of Windsor.

WHERE LIES THE SCENE?
Denmark

WHAT HAPPENS?

The king of Denmark has died, and his brother **Claudius** has assumed the throne. Claudius has hastily married his brother's queen, **Gertrude**, and **Prince Hamlet** has settled into a profound depression. Hamlet encounters the ghost of his father the king, who reveals that Claudius murdered him to attain the throne. The ghost demands vengeance. The introspective prince delays. He also pretends to be insane, apparently in an attempt to keep the king from suspecting his true intentions. The cause of Hamlet's strange disposition is the object of much discussion between the king, the queen, and the old courtier **Polonius**, who believes Hamlet to be suffering from the effects of his love for his daughter **Ophelia**. In order to test the ghost's claims, Hamlet arranges for a play mirroring the murder described by the ghost to be performed for the king. The king's reaction can leave no doubt that he did in fact commit the crime described by Hamlet's ghostly father. After the play, Hamlet confronts his mother, and, while upbraiding her for her marriage to Claudius, hears someone behind a curtain. Believing the voice to be the king's, he pulls out his sword and runs the intruder through — but he has killed the eavesdropping Polonius, not Claudius. The ghost appears again, urging Hamlet to complete his task. But this he cannot do; the king has dispatched him to England. Claudius hopes to have Hamlet killed in England, but the ship on which the prince is sailing is overtaken by pirates, who return him to his native land. When he returns to Denmark, Hamlet learns that Ophelia has gone mad and drowned. Her brother Laertes, needing no proofs or analysis before taking action, has rushed home to avenge his father's death. The king convinces Laertes to take part in a fencing match with Hamlet, rigged with a poisoned weapon to insure the prince's death. Laertes achieves his objective, poisoning the prince, but is himself mortally wounded by Hamlet with the doctored weapon. Before he dies, Hamlet sees his mother poisoned with a drink meant for him. He kills Claudius.

Keep an ear out for ongoing reference to . . .
Illness, disease (especially ulcers and tumors), food and drink, sex gone bad, words and deeds, decay.

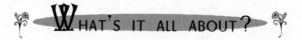

Perhaps the most critically interpreted work of literature of all time, *Hamlet* has its excesses and its baffling defects, but these tend to be, fortuitiously enough, the kinds of excesses and defects that have allowed observers to see themselves in the ambiguous figure of the prince. Hamlet is old enough to be truly brilliant, but young enough to display passionate, lightning-quick reactions. He has no tolerance for hypocrisy, yet he lies unhesitatingly, and with such confidence that we somehow find ourselves admiring him. The prince echoes our own fears when he ponders death, the "undiscover'd country, from whose bourn/No traveler returns," even though he has recently seen his own father return from that "country"! He is intelligent but ineffective, noble but profane, full of words of resolve and yet profoundly disenchanted with the purposelessness of all human action. He is all of these things (and many more) at the same time. Hamlet, the character, may be the most complicated stage effect in theatrical history. The protagonist of Shakespeare's most famous play becomes as complex as we imagine ourselves to be. In the end, he learns that even his own massive intellect cannot allow him to control his destiny or reverse the "diseases" of passing time.

℧HE CRITIC'S CORNER

"Shakespeare wished to impress upon us the truth, that action is the chief end of existence — that no faculties of intellect, however brilliant, can be considered valuable, or indeed otherwise than as misfortunes, if they withdraw us from, or render us repugnant to action . . ." (Samuel Taylor Coleridge)

"Even his instinctive sexual impules offend his intellect; so that when he meets the woman who excites them he invites her to join him in a bitter and scornful criticism of their joint absurdity . . ." (George Bernard Shaw)

"The (play) has been put togeth-er, but either there are no joints or there are so many that the creature is all curves."
(Mark Van Doren)

"The once prevalent view of Hamlet as a man who could not make up his mind because of an overly sensitive soul is no longer tenable." (Levi Fox)

LINES TO LISTEN FOR

Do not, as some ungracious pastors do,
Show me the steep and thorny way to Heaven,
Whilst, like a puff'd and reckless libertine,
Himself the primrose path of dalliance treads
And recks not his own rede(follows not his own advice). (I, iii)

. . . **I**t is a custom
More honored in the breach than the observance. (I, iv)

Something is rotten in the state of Denmark. (I, iv)

There is nothing either good or bad,
But thinking makes it so. (II, ii)

There are more things in heaven and earth, Horatio,
Than are dreamt of in your philosophy [that whole philosophy thing]. (I, v)

Brevity is the soul of wit. (II, ii)

There's hope a great man's memory may outlive his life
half a year. (III, ii)

My words fly up, my thoughts remain below;
Words without thoughts never to heaven go. (III, iii)

. . . **D**o not spread
the compost on the
weeds
To make them ranker.
(III, iv)

TO BE OR NOT TO BE, THAT IS THE QUESTION—
WHETHER 'TIS NOBLER IN THE MIND TO SUFFER
THE SLINGS AND ARROWS OF OUTRAGEOUS FORTUNE,
OR TO TAKE ARMS AGAINST A SEA OF TROUBLES,
AND BY OPPOSING END THEM?

A man may fish with the worm
that hath eat of [eaten] a king, and
eat of the fish that hath fed of
that worm. (IV, iii)

There's a divinity that shapes
our ends,
Rough-hew them how we will . . .
(V, ii)

CAMUS
SARTRE
KIERKEGAARD

Some cool things about Hamlet

5: The riddle of Hamlet's "real" reason for delaying has perplexed critics for centuries.

4: To date, Hamlet is the only Shakespearean role for which an actor has won an Academy Award. (Laurence Olivier won the Best Actor Oscar in 1948 for his performance as the melancholy Dane; his film production of Hamlet also took the Best Picture award.)

WHO AM I? OH, WELL, I'LL BE THE LAST TO KNOW—I ALWAYS AM.

3: Hamlet is the longest of Shakespeare's plays.

2: The play features a brief discussion of London's War of the Theaters (1601), in which established companies like Shakespeare's had to compete with increasingly popular troupes of boy actors. (See act II, scene ii.)

1: Hamlet's speech of Zen-like resignation in act V, scene ii ("The readiness is all.") closely parallels that of Edgar in act V, scene ii of **King Lear** ("Ripeness is all.")

WHERE LIES THE SCENE?

Troy and the Greek encampment nearby.

WHAT HAPPENS?

In the eighth year of the Greek siege of Troy, a truce has been declared. **Troilus**, one of the sons of **Priam**, the King of Troy, is in love with the Trojan maiden **Cressida**, daughter of **Calchas**, and has prevailed on the **Pandarus**, the girl's uncle, to act as go-between. The Greeks conclude that their campaign has been marred by disunity, which **Ulysses** feels arises out of insubordination. **Aeneas**, a Trojan commander, arrives bearing a challenge from **Hector**, one of Priam's sons: Hector will take on any Greek in man-to-man combat. The Greek generals slight Achilles, for whom the challenge seems to have been intended, and instead select "brainless **Ajax**" from their ranks to face Hector. The Trojans consider the Greek peace offer, which would require Helen's return and compensation via a war indemnity. Hector, who believes Helen has cost Troy far more than can be justified, argues in favor of the offer, but his brothers **Troilus**, **Paris**, and **Helenus** are against it. Their sister **Cassandra** warns of the dire consequences of further war with the Greeks, but she is ignored. Back at the Greek encampment, Achilles turns back his own generals, feigning illness in his tent. They finalize arrangements for Ajax, rather than Achilles, to fight against Hector. The deformed, misanthropic Thersites rants at anyone and anything. Pandarus arranges the meeting between Troilus and Cressida, who vow eternal love and spend the night together. The priest **Calchas**, Cressida's father, has been serving the Greek side; he asks the Greeks to exchange a Trojan prisoner, Antenor, for Cressida. The Greek generals persist in their abuse of Achilles, who is informed that he must not rest upon his laurels. Cressida's exchange for Antenor is agreed upon; Diomedes is to bring her to the Greeks. Before she and Troilus part, they again swear enternal faithfulness. Yet when she arrives at the Greek camp — where the contest between Ajax and Hector is about to begin — she instantly offers kisses to the welcoming Greek generals. The fight ends inconclusively. Troilus makes his way to the Greek camp, where he finds Cressida bestowing Troilus's own love token upon Diomedes. The next day, he seeks out Diomedes in battle — just as Menelaus, the wronged husband of Helen, seeks out Paris — but no clear victor emerges in either case. Hector kills the Greek commander Patroclus, a close friend of Achilles. Achilles, furious, rouses himself and orders his Myrmidons to kill Hector, whose body is tied to a horse's tail and dragged through Troy. Pandarus ends the play with a disconcertingly cynical epilogue.

Keep an ear out for ongoing references to . . . Honor, appetite, good, drink, foul tastes, illness, time, sex, disease.

"In *Troilus and Cressida* a disillusioned Shakespeare turns back upon his own former ideals and the world's ancient ideals of heroism and romance, and questions them. Love of woman and honor of man: Do they really exist, or are they but the thin veils which poetic sentiment has chosen to throw over the grinning realities of wantonness and egotism?" (E.K. Chambers)

"**. . . *Troilus and Cressida* is our play. . . it had to wait for cubism and atonality, for facsism and Freud.**" (R.A. Yoder)

WHAT'S IT ALL ABOUT?

Lofty words and ideals are everywhere in Troilus and Cressida. Follow-through, however, is a different matter. Cressida asks: "They that have the voices of lions and the act of hares, are they not monsters?" Her question is astute, especially considering the words and deeds of the soldiers who populate this strange but familiar world. Yet not long after she asks it, she betrays her own vows of eternal love to Troilus, and is very accommodating indeed with the Greek generals to whom she is suddenly transferred. On virtually all fronts, promise-makers turn into promise-breakers with disconcerting ease in *Troilus and Cressida*. The elaborately misanthropic Thersites appears to have the best "fix" on the chaotic surroundings. The world Shakespeare has gone to some pains to establish is one where order, fidelity, trust, and honesty simply never endure, and where pointless, honor-free bloodshed serves as a backdrop for relationships based on lies, self-interest, and short-term gain. Troilus and Cressida may not be Shakespeare's most encouraging portrait of humanity, but modern audiences familiar with military quagmires, racial butchery, and good old interpersonal alienation will find that this difficult but rewarding play mirrors many of the most troubling facets of what we assume

LINES TO LISTEN FOR

Take
but degree away,
untune that string,
And, hark, what discord
follows! (I, iii)

Love, friendship. charity, are subjects all
To envious and calumniating time. (III, iii)

O you gods divine,
Make Cressid's name the very crown of falsehood,
If ever she leave Troilus! (IV, iv)

Ulysses: May I, sweet lady, beg a kiss of you?
Cressida: You may.
Ulysses: I do desire it.
Cressida: Why, beg then. (IV, v)

O beauty, where is thy faith? (V, ii)

The bonds of heaven are slipp'd, dissolv'd, and loos'd,
And with another knot, five-finger-tied [tied by mere mortals],
The fractions of her faith, orts [scraps] of her love,
The fragments, scraps, the bits and greasy relics
Of her o'er-eaten faith, are given to Diomed. (V, ii)

O world, world, world! Thus is the poor agent (pimp) despis'd! O traders and bawds, how earnestly are you set a-work, and how ill requited! Why should our endeavor be so lov'd and the performance so loath'd? (V, x)

THYSELF UPON THYSELF! ... HEAVEN BLESS THEE FROM A TUTOR, AND DISCIPLINE COME NOT NEAR THEE. LET THY BLOOD BE THY DIRECTION TILL THY DEATH; THEN IF SHE THAT LAYS THEE OUT SAYS THOU ART A FAIR CORSE, I'LL BE SWORN AND SWORN UPON'T SHE NEVER SHROUDED ANY BUT LAZARS.
(II, iii)

8OME COOL THINGS ABOUT TROILUS AND CRESSIDA

5: The story of Cressida's betrayal came from Geoffrey Chaucer's poem *Troilus and Criseyde*.

4: Although both camps are given to exaggeration and self-deception, they have very different ways of looking at the world. The Greeks (notably Ulysses) fixate on reasoned order and hierarchies; the Trojans on chivalry and reputation.

3: In contemporary stage productions, the Greeks have been costumed as Prussian soldiers and as Nazis.

2: The play's focus on complex issues, and its less than satisfactory ending, won it the status among modern critics as one of the so-called "problem plays." (The others are usually listed as *All's Well That Ends Well* and *Measure for Measure*.)

1: The last two lines of the play give you the queebs.

THE WORLD IS ROUND AND RESISTS NEAT PACKAGING.

ALL'S WELL THAT ENDS WELL

Where lies the scene?

Rousillon, Paris, Florence, and Marseilles

What happens?

Helena, the daughter of a late, highly renowned physician, has been living with the **Countess of Rousillon,** and has fallen in love with her son Betram despite the discrepancy in their social ranks. The Countess discovers her true feelings and makes it known that the potential match is to her liking. Helena follows after **Bertram**, who has left for the royal court accompanied by the foolish and talkative **Parroles**. The young woman hopes to win favor by delivering the king from a serious illness by means of a special cure left to her by her father. · Helena arrives at court and talks the reluctant king into trying her cure. He is restored to health in only two days, and enthusiastically promises to grant Helena any request. She asks, and is granted permission, to choose a husband from among the bachelors in attendance, but when she selects Bertram, the young man refuses the match. The King demands that Helena's wish be fulfilled, and orders the marriage rites performed immediately. They are, but Bertram leaves for the battlefield before the union can be consummated. Helena, back at home with the Countess, receives a letter from Bertram informing her that he will not return to France until Helena can obtain his ancestral ring and show him a child to whom he is the father. The same news has been passed along to the Countess. Distraught, Helena makes her way to St. Jacques de Grand as a pilgrim. Bertram, who has performed honorably in battle, returns to Florence at the same time that Helena, dressed as a Pilgrim, arrives in the city.

Word of her death reaches Roussilon. Helen learns from a Florentine widow who provides her with shelter that Bertram has designs on the widow's daughter **Diana**. Helena reveals her identity to the pair, and promises Diana a dowry if she will obtain Bertram's ring, arrange a tryst with him — and then allow Helena to sleep with him instead. Diana wins the ring and sets up the rendezvous. Helena takes her place and sleeps with her husband in Diana's place, providing Bertram with a ring given to her by the king. Parolles is proven to be a liar, a coward, and a braggart. Bertram heads back to Rousillon when he receives a letter from his mother passing along word of Helena's supposed death. The king visits the Countess, who begs the monarch to forgive her son's many transgressions. Bertram, seemingly reconciled with the king, is about to be married to the daughter of the old lord Lafeu when the king notices on Bertram's finger the ring that he, the king, gave to Helena. Bertram sputters out explanations, but when Diana and her mother appear demanding that Bertram marry Diana, the king loses his temper. Bertram is disgraced again, and the evasive Diana is sent off to prison, but Helena, who had been thought dead, reappars and resolves the many questions in the court. She has fulfilled the conditions of Bertram's letter, as she now has his ring and is carrying his child. Bertram apologizes for his past actions and swears to love Helena "ever dearly."

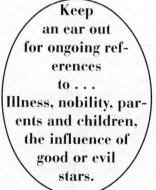

YOUR HIGHNESS THIS SHOULD FIX YOU RIGHT UP.

Keep an ear out for ongoing references to . . . Illness, nobility, parents and children, the influence of good or evil stars.

☾ WHAT'S IT ALL ABOUT? ☾

All's Well that Ends Well offers some memorable character portraits: the healing, forgiving Helena, whom many have identified as a source of grace and unremitting love; the noble Countess; and the fast-talking, hypocritical Parolles, who stands in as a fairly rewarding Falstaff substitute. But for many, the play is unsatisfying. This is due in part to a decision of Shakespeare's to make the character of Bertram less likeable than he might be — and, interestingly, less likeable than his counterpart in the source story by Boccaccio. · The eventual marriage between Helena and Bertram has left generations of theatergoers scratching their heads and wondering what on earth the "virtuous gentlewoman" sees in the bounder; the final scene highlights many difficulties in the script. A certain cynicism on Shakespeare's part about the limits of comdedy itself isn't hard to detect in the play's later scenes. (The same cynicism reappears a year or so later in *Measure for Measure*.)

"I cannot reconcile my heart to Bertram; a man noble without generosity, and young without truth . . ."
(Samuel Johnson)

"Few can read, or see, the play with any hope of the possibility of happiness in a couple so married." (John Masefield)

"(It examines love) from the oblique angle of maturity." (Josephine Bennett)

LINES TO LISTEN FOR

In delivering my son from me I bury a second husband. (I, i)

Our remedies oft in ourselves do lie,
Which we ascribe to heaven. (I, i)

It is in us to plant thine honor where
We please to have it grow. (II, iii)

THE WEB OF LIFE IS OF A MINGLED YARN,
GOOD AND ILL TOGETHER. (IV, iii)

I know I love in vain, strive against hope;
Yet in this captious (accepting) and intenable (porous) sieve,
I still (always) pour in the waters of my love
And lack not to lose still. Thus, Indian-like,
Religious in mine error, I adore
The sun, that looks upon his worshipper
But knows of him no more. (I, iii)

How mightily sometimes we make us comforts
of our losses. (IV, iii)

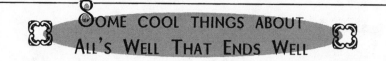

5: The play's focus on complex issues, and its less than satisfactory ending, won it the status among modern critics as one of the so-called "problem plays." (The others are usually listed as *Troilus and Cressida* and *Measure for Measure*.)

4: A decision on Shakespeare's part to highlight uncomfortable, even unattractive truths is clear in the king's infirmity, a fistula — defined in modern dictionaries as "an abnormal tubelike passage from one abscess or cavity to another."

3: The play focuses more strongly and frankly on sexual matters than many of the earlier comedies, often in a strangely disconcerting way. (See Helena's discussion with Parolles about virginity in act I, scene i.)

2: Tension between words and later actions is a running theme in All's Well.

1: Considering the unusually — and deliberately? — unsatisfying conclusion, many critics have wondered whether the title of the play represents an ironic comment of sorts from Shakespeare.

IRONY? MY, THAT'S A BIT SOPHISTICATED FOR ME DON'T YOU THINK?

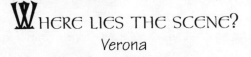

WHERE LIES THE SCENE?
Verona

WHAT HAPPENS?

Duke Vincentio, hoping to encourage moral reform and adherence to justice, arranges to leave the city and transfer its management to **Lord Angelo** and the counselor **Escalus.** Angelo revives an old law that requires fornicators to be put to death. The young **Claudio,** who has unlawfully slept with and impregnated his fiancee **Juliet,** is to be made an example and put to death. On his way to captivity, Claudio implores his friend **Lucio** to get Claudio's sister **Isabella,** who is entering a convent, to plead his cause before Angelo. We learn that the Duke is still in Verona, disguised as a friar, monitoring Angelo and Escalus. Neither Escalus nor a Justice can persuade Angelo to spare Claudio's life; Isabella's pleas also seem to fall on deaf ears. But the lovely novice stirs Angelo's passions, and when the two meet for the second time he suggests that her brother's life could be saved . . . if Isabella will yield her virginity to him. Shocked, she refuses. The disguised Duke visits Claudio in prison and is convinced that his love for Juliet is true. Isabella visits her brother in prison and informs him that she will not save his life if doing so means yielding to Angelo. After a tense exchange, Claudio is led away, and the disguised Duke, who has been listening to the interview, makes his presence known and shares a plan with Isabella that will allow her to save her brother's life. The scheme requires Isabella to appear to yield to Angelo by scheduling a midnight tryst. In her place, however, Mariana, Angelo's betrothed — and jilted — former love, will sleep with him. After Angelo has had his way with the maid he believes to be Isabella, he reneges on the agreement and orders Claudio beheaded, demanding that the head be sent directly to him. The disguised Duke convinces the Provost to send Angelo the head of another criminal who has died of natural causes. He does not inform Isabella of his actions, allowing her to believe her brother has been executed. The "friar" also suggests that Isabella make her case known to the Duke, who is, he explains, to return to Verona the next day. · Angelo, Escalus, and other officers of Verona meet the Duke at the gates of the city. There, Isabella accuses Angelo of murder and licentiousness. The Duke excuses himself, hands the case to Angelo, and returns as the friar, in which role he provides testimony that supports both Isabel and Mariana. His credibility is assailed, but when his cowl is removed and he is recognized as the Duke, the whole truth is revealed. Angelo is sentenced to death, but the Duke revokes the penalty at the urging of both Isabella and Mariana. Claudio and Juliet are married. As the play ends, the Duke makes an appeal for Isabella's hand.

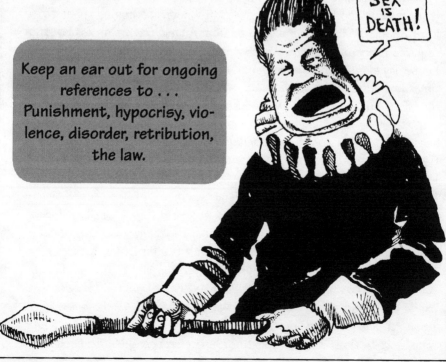

Keep an ear out for ongoing references to . . .
Punishment, hypocrisy, violence, disorder, retribution, the law.

SEX IS DEATH!

What's it all about?

In this play, as in *All's Well That Ends Well*, Shakespeare seems to have decided to highlight, rather than de-emphasize, limitations of the comic form. The result is a fascinating look at extremity and hypocrisy. This is a complicated drama that seems, at times, to provoke its audience deliberately.

No production of the play can ever make the sudden romantic overture of the Duke to Isabella in the fifth act appear believable — or even satisfyingly unbelievable as a fairy-tale resolution. Is the sudden pairing a slip on Shakespeare's part, or is it one of many unusual, but conscious, artistic choices in an oddly abrasive play about brothels, moral lapses, betrayal, executions, and a raft of other sordid city problems? This is an urban universe where betrayal and disappointment are unavoidable . . . and where there are no enchanted forests, as there are in *A Midsummer Night's Dream*.

The Critics' Corner

"It is a hateful work, although Shakespearian throughout. Our feelings of justice are grossly wounded in Angelo's escape. Isabella herself contrives to be unamiable, and Claudio is detestable." (Samuel Taylor Coleridge)

"Within the religion she professes Isabella's position seems secure, but the play, like the world, is filled with competing ethical systems which are not necessarily compatible, and Shakespeare evidently expected his audience to consider carefully the heavy ethical weight placed upon her by this situation." (Levi Fox)

LINES TO LISTEN FOR

Heaven doth with us as we with torches do,
Not light them for themselves; for if our virtues
Did not go forth of us, 'twere all alike
As if we had them not. (I, i)

Truth is truth,
To the end of reck-oning. (V, i)

SOME RISE BY SIN,
SOME BY VIRTUE FALL.
(II, i)

Our doubts are traitors,
And make us lose the good we oft might win
By fearing to attempt. (I, iv)

It is excellent
To have a giant's strength, but it is tyrannous
To use it like a giant. (II, ii)

. . . man, proud man,
Dress'd in a little brief authority . . .
(II, ii)

O, what may man within him hide,
Though angel on the outward hide! (III, ii)

8ome cool things about Measure for Measure

5: The play's focus on complex issues, and its less than satisfactory ending, won it the status among modern critics as one of the so-called "problem plays." (The others are usually listed as *Troilus and Cressida* and *All's Well That Ends Well*.)

4: Angelo's name iswell chosen. He projects a public image of himself that is beyond human passion and temptation — angelic — but he proves to be all too human.

3: *Measure for Measure* places an unusually intense emphasis on the divide between heavenly standards and human performance.

2: The executioner Abhorson's name appears to be a combination of the words "abhor" and "whoreson."

I: In many of the comedies, Shakespeare emphasizes some kind of physical triumph over a representative of Death. In *Measure for Measure*, as though parodying this earlier thematic device, he makes a point of working a severed head into the stage action in full view of the audience (see act IV, scene iii).

PROBLEMS — I'LL GIVE YOU PROBLEMS. LIFE ... THERE YOU GO WITH PROBLEMS.

WHERE LIES THE SCENE?
Britain in the century before the birth of Christ.

WHAT HAPPENS?

Lear, the old king, plans to divide the realm among his three daughters, then retire in honor. He sets up an elaborate game in which each daughter is required to proclaim her love publicly; **Goneril** and **Regan** consent, and offer flattering declarations of affection, but **Cordelia**, who actually loves Lear the most of the three, protests. She argues that her sisters, who have husbands whom they claim to love, must be deceiving the King when they swear that they adore him with all their being. Furious, Lear rashly disowns Cordelia and splits the territory that had been meant for her between the two older sisters. He also exiles **the Earl of Kent** when he attempts to defend Cordelia. The youngest daughter, deprived of her dowry, is claimed by **the King of France**, and must leave the kingdom. In a subplot that closely parallels the main action of the play, the cunning **Edmund**, illegitimate son of the trusting **Earl of Gloucester**, fools his father into exiling **Edgar**, Gloucester's rightful heir. Goneril and Regan strip away all vestiges of the King's authority, leaving him bereft of his royal retinue — and his identity. Lear, powerless and increasingly unstable, is left without shelter to face a horrific storm with only Kent (who, in disguising himself, has risked his life to serve the King) and the Fool. The trio encounters a babbling madman — actually, Edgar in disguise. Lear, who has gone mad, is led to safety by Gloucester. Edmund betrays his father, whose eyes are torn out by the **Duke of Cornwall** in one of the most ghastly scenes in theatrical history. Blind and alone, the suicidal Gloucester is befriended by a seeming madman — in reality his son Edgar, whom he does not recognize. Cordelia, who has returned with a French military force, is reunited with her father. A tearful Lear shows a new and hard-won humility. The two are captured when the French forces falter against the English. Edmund, Goneril, and Regan have won the day, but their all-pervasive wickedness turns victory into defeat. The sisters, rivals for Edmund's affections, destroy each other: Goneril murders Regan, then kills herself. Edmund is vanquished by a triumphant Edgar. Lear enters, carrying the innocent Cordelia in his arms; Edmund had ordered her hanged. Lear dies. Edgar assumes control of the kingdom..

KEEP AN EYE OUT FOR ONGOING REFERENCES TO: **Vision, nature, the gods, clothing, nakedness, authority; foolishness, nothingness, sundered and divided bodies, torture.**

WHAT'S IT ALL ABOUT?

Brutal, awe-inspiring, blood-spattered and occasionally unendurable, *King Lear* provides a sweeping landscape of world-shaking generational conflict and miscalculation. The two massive plot lines that tell virtually the same tale; its characters inhabit an apocalyptic world that has seemingly been abandoned by the gods who should control it. This is a terrifying universe where any semblance of order has been undermined, and where agonizing acts of cruelty by children toward parents, by guests toward hosts, and by subjects toward the sovereign are commonplace. The play's most monstrous acts are blithely dismissed by perpetrators eager to move on to fresh conquests. Lear's hellish storms are set off by acts of human egotism and imperiousness, hideous errors in judgment by men who should know better. Once the initial mistakes are made, however, the action of the drama is fueled by villains whose inhumanity is terrifying not just of its suddenness and violence, but also of its disconcerting familiarity. King Lear's errors and attendant sufferings lead the sitting monarch to madness (a truly terrifying idea for Shakespeare's audience). The agonizing path he follows past the boundaries of sanity brings him to a long-overdue reassessment of his notion of self. The once-haughty king experiences life not as an independent exercise in the exertion of an all-powerful will, but as a fading gift valuable only as it relates to others. Even with this discovery, the malignant powers that have been unleashed are too powerful to be contained. Lear, though remade, must forfeit his kingdom, his daughter, and, finally, his own life, for his folly.

SOMETIMES MADNESS IS THE ONLY SANE REACTION.

The critics' corner:

"(The play's) final and total result is one in which pity and terror, carried perhaps to the extreme limits of art, are so blended with a sense of law and beauty that we feel at last, not depression and much less despair, but a consciousness of greatness in pain, and of solemnity in the mystery we cannot fathom." (A.C. Bradley)

"What the play means, it means all of the time, which must be the last way now of saying that it is not only wide but deep, not only pitiful but huge." (Mark Van Doren)

"All that remains at the end of this gigantic pantomime, is the earth — empty and bleeding." (Carol Gesner)

LINES TO LISTEN FOR

Nothing will come of nothing. (I, i)

... **H**e hath ever but slenderly known himself. (I, ii.)

Oh, you, sir, you, come you hither, sir. Who am I, sir? (I, iv)

How [much] sharper than a serpent's tooth it is
To have a thankless child! (I. iv)

Poor naked wretches, wheresoe'er you are,
That bide [abide] the pelting of this pitiless storm,
How shall your houseless heads and
unfed sides,
Your loop'd and window'd ragged-
ness, defend you
From seasons such as these? O, I
have ta'en
Too little care of this! Take
physic [medicine], pomp;
Expose thyself to feel what
wretches feel,
That thou mays shake the
superflux [extra] to them,
And show the heavens [to be]
more just. (III, iv)

... THE TEMPEST IN MY MIND DOTH FROM MY SENSES TAKE ALL FEELINGS ELSE SAVE WHAT BEAT THERE. (III, iv)

Is man no more than this? Consider
him well. Thou ow'st the worm no silk, the
beast no hide, the sheep no wool, the cat no perfume. Ha! Here three on's [of us] are sophisticated, [but]
thou art the thing itself! Unaccommodated man is no more than
such a poor, bare, forked animal as thou art. (III, iv)

As flies to wanton boys are we to the gods;
They kill us for their sport. (IV, i)

What, in ill thoughts again? Men must endure
Their going hence, even as their coming hither;
Ripeness is all. (V, ii)

8OME COOL THINGS ABOUT KING LEAR

5: It's about, among other things, the end of the world. Twentieth-century audiences turned out to be the first since Shakespeare's time to be willing to watch it as it was written. (Previously, a happy ending, in which Lear and Cordelia lived, was hammered on.)

4: The Fool, a brilliant comic creation who also serves to provide an ironic running commentary on Lear's ruin, vanishes for no particular reason. (Lear's line late in the play about his poor fool having been hanged refers to Cordelia.)

DON'T WORRY YOU AIN'T NEVER FAR FROM THE FOOL.

3: Lear's early speeches are regal, stilted, formal, and framed around Latin-based words. (For instance, in the first scene of Act One: "Here I disclaim all my paternal care, / Propinquity and propriety of blood . . .".) By the end of the piece, the phrasing is simple and direct, and the words he uses are primarily Anglo-Saxon in origin. ("Pray you undo this button. Thank you, sir./ Do you see this? Look on her!" [V, iii])

2: Edmund's materialistic outlook, which sets great store on determining one's own fate, and glories in the choice to let human will serve personal desire, resembles Iago's in *Othello*.

1: Chaos happens and the gods (remember, this is a story set in a polytheistic, pre-Christian era) don't much care. Immediately after Albany's line appealing to the higher forces to save Cordelia — "The gods defend her" (V, iii) — Lear enters holding her dead body in his arms.

WHERE LIES THE SCENE?
Venice and Cyprus

WHAT HAPPENS?

Othello, a noble Moor who has failed to grant Iago a sought-after promotion, has secretly married **Desdemona**, daughter of the Venetian senator **Brabantio**. Iago and the dull-witted **Roderigo**, who pines for Desdemona, awaken Brabantio in the middle of the night and alert the girl's father to the elopement. During an emergency session convened by the Venetian Senate to address an imminent attack by the Turks on Cyprus, Brabantio appears and claims that Othello has stolen his daughter away by means of witchcraft. The Senate, after hearing Othello's explanation of the courtship, rejects Brabantio's claim. Othello is dispatched to Cyprus to put down the Turks; he appoints the "honest" Iago to bring Desdemona on another ship. **Roderigo** accompanies Iago, under the impression that he will somehow gain Desdemona's favor by following Iago's instructions. A storm undoes the Turkish fleet, and Othello, the island's new governor, arrives at Cyprus in triumph. He orders a holiday to celebrate both the passage of danger and his own marriage. In charge of the events: **Michael Cassio**, the man who won the promotion Iago had desired. Iago determines to find a way to make Othello believe that Desdemona has been unfaithful to him, and has been having an affair with Cassio. Iago encourages Cassio to get drunk. Roderigo, following Iago's instructions, picks a fight with Cassio. The altercation disturbs the general, who demands a full accounting of the strange scene. Iago, feigning reluctance, provides the details, and Cassio is demoted. Iago suggests that Cassio ask Desdemona to act on his behalf and help him regain his standing with the general. Cassio agrees. Later, Othello observes the end of a meeting between Cassio and Desdemona. Iago makes the most of Cassio's hasty departure from Desdemona, and implies that there is something untoward in the way the two conduct themselves. Iago sets many and varied traps for the general. He tells Othello to be wary if Desdemona should attempt to speak in Cassio's favor. (She does.) Othello's reason begins to give way to jealousy. Following Iago's line of suggestion, Othello asks Desdemona to produce a favored handkerchief he gave to her

HEY, OTHELLO, DESDEMONA SEEMS MIGHTY INTERESTED IN CASSIO — AND I DON'T MEAN CHEAP ELECTRONICS.

during their courtship. (Iago has snatched it up himself after his wife found the lost article.) She cannot. Othello is convinced that his wife is faithless. After Iago arranges a dangerous game in which Othello listens to a conversation about Cassio's mistress, and assumes that he is speaking about Desdemona, Othello commits to kill his wife. Before he can do this, however, he must deal with a Venetian delegation recalling Othello from Cyprus. Desdemona mentions Cassio's predicament and her hope that it can be resolved; Othello strikes her in full view of the delegation. Later, he torments the innocent young woman in private with some very menacing talk of whores and whorehouses. Iago persuades the foolish Roderigo to attempt to murder Cassio. In the event, Roderigo only wounds him. Othello suffocates his wife in their bed. Iago's wife Emilia realizes the extent of her husband's villainy, but the truth is brought to the surface too late. Othello attempts to kill Iago, but only wounds him. Othello then kills himself. Cassio assumes the duties of governor.

KEEP AN EAR OPEN FOR ONGOING REFERENCES TO . . .

Animals, threats to the stability of the state, frontier outposts, torture, foul smells.

What's it all about?

Many critics have argued that Othello, while it deals with sexual jealousy, is actually a play about society at large. Like Measure for Measure, it looks intensely at obstacles to harmonious communities. There are perils and hazards at the outermost reaches of civilization (i.e., Cyprus, rather than Venice), where the relationships that hold a town together — marriage, for instance — are subject to attack by people who ruthlessly pursue selfishness. Iago is such a person; like a number of Shakespeare's most effective villains, he all but worships the Self. Iago's opposite, Desdemona, exemplifies not egotism, but trusting and total love. The two are engaged in a battle of sorts for control of the soul of Othello, who is "of a free and open nature," and "thinks men honest that but seem to be so." The play works as a drama of jealousy, of course, but on another level it is a tragic reworking of themes from the old morality plays. A brilliant egotist (Iago) attacks a noble, brave man (Othello) at his very weakest point. The figure of Vice wins the honorable man over to his brand of obsessive self-absorption, and to the lie that the embodiment of love and altruism in his life (Desdemona) is in fact inherently false and destructive. In the fall of Othello, a man for whom service to the state was nearly everything, the basic human trust on which any society has to be based collapses.

EXTRA! EXTRA! READ ALL ABOUT IT! BARBARIANS ATTACK— AND THEY ARE US!

THE DAILY GLOBE BARBARIANS ATTACK!

The critics' corner

"The beauties of this play impress themselves so strongly upon the attention of the reader, that they can draw no aid from critical illustration." (Samuel Johnson) "(Iago's) motive-hunting of motiveless malignity — how awful!" (Samuel Taylor Coleridge) "Not Socrates himself, not the ideal sage of the Stoics, was more lord of himself than Iago seems to be." (A.C. Bradley) "(O)ne can isolate a plot of monumental and satisfying simplicity without forgetting that the text can be made to support very differing interpretations." (Frank Kermode)

LINES TO LISTEN FOR

Why, how now ho? From whence ariseth this?
Are we turn'd Turks, and to ourselves do that
Which heaven hath forbid the Ottomites? (II, iii)

O, beware, my lord, of jealousy;
It is the green-ey'd monster which
doth mock
The meat it feeds on. (III, iii)

EVEN NOW, NOW, VERY NOW, AN OLD BLACK RAM
IS TUPPING YOUR WHITE EWE. ARISE, ARISE!
(I, i)

Who steals my purse steals trash . . .
But he that filches from me my good name
Robs me of that which not enriches him,
And makes me poor indeed. (III, iii)

Set you down this;
And say besides, that in
Aleppo once,
Where a malignant and a
turbann'd Turk
Beat a Venetian and tra-
duc'd the state,
I took by th' throat the cir-
cumcised dog,
And smote him — thus. [He
stabs himself.]

O thou weed,
Who art so lovely
fair and smells't so
sweet
That the sense
aches at thee, would
thou hadst ne'er
been born! (IV, ii)

SOME COOL THINGS ABOUT OTHELLO

5: Many ideas have been tossed around concerning Iago's "motivation" for tempting and tormenting Othello in the first place. The villain himself provides a good many theories, perhaps too many. For some reason, actors have less of a problem with this issue than critics do.

4: The play features two simultaneous, and contrasting, sets of time references: one that allows for a (classical) compression of time and gives the impression that once the scene changes to Cyprus, the action unfolds in a matter of a day or two, and another that allows Desdemona to have had enough time to have actually conducted an affair with Michael Cassio in Cyprus after her wedding night.

3: Othello's refusal to believe Desdemona has been compared to a failure of religious faith — an excessive reliance on reason and apparent rationality.

2: Iago's use of coarse sexual imagery throughout the play — particularly images involving animals — underlines his inability to see love in anything other than carnal terms. After Iago has broken down Othello's will, the general begins to use the same language.

1: Othello's final act — suicide — is a conscious choice on his part to execute a man (himself) whom he realizes to be an enemy to the welfare of the city of Venice.

Where lies the scene?
Eleventh-century Scotland and England

What happens?

Three witches meet the generals **Macbeth** and **Banquo** after they have fought bravely and put down an uprising by **Macdonwald** and the **thane (baron) of Cawdor**. The witches hail Macbeth as the thane of **Glamis** (a title Macbeth now possesses), thane of Cawdor, and future King of Scotland. Banquo asks what the future holds for him, and is told that, although he will not be king, his descendants will. The witches vanish. Almost immediately, Macbeth learns that the thane of Cawdor is to be executed, and he, Macbeth, is to assume his land and title. Macbeth takes the incomplete fulfillment of the witches' prophecies, and **King Duncan's** decision to name his son **Malcolm Prince of Cumberland**, as reason to plot the death of the king. At his own castle, he hesitates as the time for the planned murder of the visiting Duncan approaches, but his wife **Lady Macbeth** insists that they carry the deed through. Lady Macbeth drugs the grooms who guard the king's room. Macbeth, after an agony of deliberation, murders Duncan. The arrival of the nobleman **Macduff** leads to the discovery of the King's body and the awakening of all in the castle; when the grooms deny having killed the king, Macbeth slaughters them as well. The king's sons, in fear of their own lives, flee Scotland. Macbeth assumes the throne. Macbeth realizes that Banquo suspects him of Duncan's murder, and recalls the witches' prophecy that Banquo's progeny would become kings. He invites Banquo to a formal dinner, but arranges for thugs to attack him and his son **Fleance** before the event. Banquo is killed; Fleance escapes. During the dinner, Macbeth — and no one else in attendance — sees the bloody ghost of Banquo. The gathering parts in chaos. Malcolm, Duncan's eldest son, meets with Macduff, who has fled Scotland for England. Macbeth seeks out the witches, and is shown a series of strange visions; the witches explain that the king should beware Macduff, but vow that "none of woman born" will harm Macbeth. They also promise that he will be safe until he sees the forest at Birnam Wood rise against him. In reprisal against Macduff, Macbeth orders the nobleman's wife and children murdered. Malcolm and Macduff resolve to join forces against Macbeth. Macduff is informed that his family has perished. Lady Macbeth, racked with guilt, loses her sanity. Macbeth makes ready to do battle with the English. To make estimates of the size of their force more difficult, the English soldiers march with boughs cut from trees in Birnam Wood, making it appear the forest is moving. This intelligence is conveyed to Macbeth, as is the fact that his Queen has died. Macbeth resolves to fight the battle out. In time, he is confronted by Macduff. Macbeth boasts that no man born of woman can slay him; Macduff informs his adversary that he was not born of woman. Instead, he was "from his mother's womb untimely ripp'd." Macduff kills the usurping king; Malcolm ascends to the throne.

WHAT'S IT ALL ABOUT?

Although Macbeth is a willing pursuant of choices that lead to his own downfall, the sickening downward ride he endures picks up speed at such an exponential rate that he wins an almost unexpected sympathy. The guiding word in Macbeth is "fear." Not only Macbeth, but virtually every character of note in the story is forced to confront something terrifying. Terror is on display in some form or another in the play almost from beginning to end. The second scene of the play, which is filled with bloody reports of "things strange" on the battlefield, offers an image that perfectly captures the destructive action of fear in Macbeth: the two exhausted swimmers who cling to each other and hasten their own drowning. The entire play is a dark symphony of fear and miscalculation.

> Keep an ear out for ongoing references to . . .
> Blood, garments (especially ones that do not fit
> Macbeth), equivocation, echoes, light overcome by
> darkness, sleeplessness

THE CRITICS' CORNER

"(A)lmost all the scenes which at once recur to memory take place either at night or in some dark spot." (A.C. Bradley)

"(Macbeth presents) Shakespeare's most profound and mature vision of Evil." (G. Wilson Knight.)

"It is certainly indicative that there are only two plays in which the word 'love' occurs so seldom as in Macbeth, and no play in which 'fear' occurs so often; indeed, it occurs twice or thrice as often as in most other plays." (Caroline Spurgeon)

LINES TO LISTEN FOR

Vaulting ambition, which o'erleaps itself
And falls on the other side. (I, vii)

Fair is foul
and foul is fair.
(I, i)

Doubtful it stood;
As two spent swimmers, that do cling together
And choke their art . . . (I, ii)

. . . good things of day begin to droop and drowse. (III, ii)

DOUBLE, DOUBLE TOIL AND TROUBLE; FIRE BURN AND CAULDRON BUBBLE. (IV, i)

List'ning their fear, I could not say "Amen,"
When they did say "God bless us."
. .
But wherefore could I not pronounce "Amen"?
I had most need of blessing, and "Amen"
Stuck in my throat. (II, ii)

Tomorrow, and tomorrow, and tomorrow,
Creeps in this petty pace from day to day,
To the last syllable of recorded time . . . (V, 5)

Macbeth shall never vanquish'd be until
Great Birnam wood to high Dunsinane hill
Shall come against him. (IV, iii)

S⊕ⱲE C⊕⊕L ✝HINGS AB⊕U✝
ⱲACBE✝H

5: The play celebrates the accession to the English throne of James I, whose Scottish lineage and interest in the supernatural appear to have been important factors in Shakespeare's selection of materials.

4: Theatrical legend has it that the play is cursed. A good many actors will not speak the name of the play within the confines of a theater unless a scene being performed or rehearsed requires them to do so.

> MACBETH, I MEAN, THE SCOTTISH PLAY CURSED? I'VE NEVER HEARD SUCH NONSENSE.

3: As usual, Shakespeare doesn't let historical details get in the way of a good story. The actual Macbeth reigned for seventeen years and had considerable popular support. Duncan, whom he slew in battle, was a young man.

2: The only text for Macbeth appears in the First Folio of 1623. It may feature scenes from another writer, added at some point after Shakespeare completed the play (perhaps 1606). The witch sequences appearing in act III, scene v, and parts of act IV, scene i, are thought by many to be non-Shakespearean.

1: For an Elizabethan audience, the murder of a king — and, what's more, a king who is a guest in the household of his assailant — was more than "assassination." It was among the most horrific crimes imaginable, similar to, say, incest or the murder of a parent.

ANTONY + CLEOPATRA

WHERE LIES THE SCENE?

Alexandria, Rome, Messina, Athens, Misenum, Actium, and elsewhere in the Roman Empire

WHAT HAPPENS?

In Alexandria, the general **Mark Antony**, with **Octavius** and **Lepidus** one of three members of the ruling Triumvirate, has become distracted by the Egyptian queen **Cleopatra** (former lover of **Julius Caesar**). Antony's Roman followers in Alexandria worry about the change in the general's character. Word reaches Antony of difficulties in Rome, of an accumulating sea force under young **Pompey**, who seeks vengeance for his father's death, and of the dealth of Antony's wife **Fulvia**. Antony snaps to and returns to Rome. In Rome, after harsh words, Antony and the young Octavius re-establish their ties. Antony agrees to marry Octavius's sister Octavia. The conflict with Pompey is resolved. A magnificent feast takes place aboard one of Pompey's vessels. Antony, after an encounter with a soothsayer, is privately convinced that his interests are not served by union with Caesar, and sends Ventidius on a military campaign into Parthia. Enobarbus predicts that Antony will return to his Egyptian lover, with dire consequeces. In

Egypt, Cleopatra takes the news of Antony's marriage badly. Some time afterwards, Cleopatra contents herself with reports that Octavia's physical charms are insufficient to hold Antony. Ventidius's Parthian campaign results in victory; Antony travels with his new wife to Athens. When he arrives, he receives messages that make it clear that there is new trouble between himself and Octavius, who has resumed the conflict with Pompey without allowing Antony a place in the campaign. Octavius has also imprisoned Lepidus, the third member of the Triumvirate, removing him from power. Octavia proposes that her husband allow her to return to Rome to mend fences, and Antony agrees. Even before Octavius's sister enters Rome, however, people are buzzing with the news that Antony has returned to Alexandria and Cleopatra. Octavius makes preparations for war against Antony. Despite the sound advice of his officers, Antony resolves to battle Octavius at sea and is defeated. He falls further under the influence of the Egyptian Queen, who is responsible at least in part for his military loss. Antony tries to secure favorable terms, but is rebuffed. A Roman ambassador very nearly succeeds in turning Cleopatra against Antony, but when Antony discovers the effort he has the man whipped and returns him to Rome with a challenging message. After the incident, Cleopatra wins back Antony's affections with ease. Antony's followers abandon his cause and unite with Octavius. In the ensuing battle, Antony's force is at first successful on land, but the surrender of Egypt's fleet leaves him looking at utter defeat. Furious, and suspecting Cleopatra of treachery, he vows to take the queen's life. She retires to her monument and circulates a rumor that she died speaking Antony's name. Antony receives word of this and is distraught, begging his companion Eros to kill him. Eros commits suicide rather than carry out the order, at which Antony falls on his sword. Word reaches him that Cleopatra is not in fact dead; he asks to be taken to her. Although she will not risk her own safety by descending from the monument to meet her lover, the queen has Antony hoisted up to her, where he dies in her embrace. · Under heavy guard, Cleopatra learns that she is to be led to Rome as a prisoner and jeered at by the common people as part of Octavius's triumphal procession. She displays a newfound dignity and serenity as she takes an asp that has been smuggled to her in a basket of figs, allows it to bite her breast, and perishes. Octavius orders that she be buried in the same grave as Antony.

Keep an ear out for ongoing references to . . . Worlds, immensity and vastness, sex and death (note: "dying" is often an Elizabethan term for orgasm), love, duty.

WHAT'S IT ALL ABOUT?

This is a lavish, mature, and occasionally ironic contrast to *Romeo and Juliet*. The young lovers of Verona give up everything for their newfound (and short-lived) passion. Their older counterparts find that grownup love is both more complex and more ennobling. The Egyptian queen makes a point of not leaving her sanctuary when the time comes to kiss the dying Antony one last time. The great Roman is lifted up to her to say his farewell. Everything about the play is expansive: its scope, its construction, its stakes, its plot, its heroes, and its unparalled language. In selecting the world he will embrace — the world of love, embodied in the fertile, captivating enchantment of Cleopatra and her Egypt, or the world of duty, represented by the Rome of Octavius — Antony makes a choice that calls the simplistic, opportunistic Roman view of reality into question. Whether the choice he makes is morally defensible (or logical) seems not to be the point. In Cleopatra, there is more than passion. There is divinity.

QUEEN OF EGYPT, LOVER OF CAESER, ANTONY, AND ALL IT COMES TO: AN ASP BITE.

THE CRITICS' CORNER

"(T)he sense of criminality in [Cleopatra's] passion is lessened by our insight into its depth and energy, at the very moment that we cannot but perceive that the passion itself springs out of the habitual craving of a licentious nature . . ." (Samuel Taylor Coleridge)

"In Plutarch Antony lives long with Octavia, in Shakespeare the marriage was a mere formality. Who does not see in this perversion of history, by the hand of a genius, a feature of exquisite delicacy? The poet would not suffer his hero to be for a single instant unfaithful to his heroine. He has not permitted a single treason, even if legalized, to profane this sanctified adultery." (Victor Hugo)

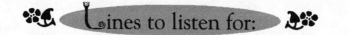
(H) is captain's heart,
Which in the scuffles of great fights hath burst
The buckles on his breast, reneges all temper,
And is become the bellows and the fan
To cool a gipsy's lust. (I,i)

Her (Cleopatra's) passions are made of nothing but the finest part of pure love. We cannot call her winds and waters sighs and tears; they are greater storms and tempests than almanacs can report. (I, ii)

Age cannot wither her nor custom stale
Her infinite variety. Other women cloy
The appetites they feed, but she makes hungry
Where most she satisfies; for vilest things
Become themselves [take on a becoming appearance] in her. (II, ii)

Let's have one other gaudy night. (III, xiii)

My salad days,
When I was green in judgment. (I, v)

⊕, wither'd is the garland of the war,
The soldier's pole (standard) is falln'n! Young boys and girls
Are level now with men; the odds is gone,
And there is nothing left remarkable
Beneath the visiting moon . . . (IV, xv)

The stroke of death is as a lover's
pinch,
Which hurts, and is desir'd. (V,
ii)

Peace, peace!
Dost thou not see my baby at my breast
That sucks the nurse asleep? (V, ii)

MOM WAS RIGHT. YOU SHOULDN'T RUN WITH SHARP OBJECTS.

SOME COOL THINGS ABOUT ANTONY AND CLEOPATRA

5: Cleopatra is one of the world's great theatrical parts, and is generally considered to be Shakespeare's most demanding female lead role. (And a man originated the role!)

4: The play's thematic struggle between love and duty — the private self in conflict with the public self — occasionally takes the form of rapid scene shifts.

3: Many critics (including George Bernard Shaw) seem to have taken the remarks of Philo in play's opening scene as the moral yardstick against which Antony's behavior should be judged, but this is a simplistic approach. Once again, Shakespeare seems willing to allows the audience to draw its own conclusions.

ME — PLAYED BY A MAN! I DON'T THINK SO!

2: Competing definitions of "the world" run throughout the play. The word "world" appears over forty times in the text.

1: Many consider Antony and Cleopatra to represent the highest dramatic example of Shakespeare's mature poetic style.

WHERE LIES THE SCENE?

Rome, Corioles, Antium, and their environs

WHAT HAPPENS?

The starving citizens of Rome mount a revolt against the Senate, focusing much of their ire on the arrogant but noble general **Caius Marcius**. The elderly patrician **Meninius Agrippa** attempts to use skillful rhetoric to defuse the passions of the hungry throng. The blunt Marcius, however, makes no effort to conceal his disgust at the mob's low character. While he harangues the citizens, word arrives that wars against the Volsces and Marcius's supreme rival, **Tullus Aufidius**, require the general's departure for Corioli. **Volumnia**, Marcius's proud mother, sees in her son's departure the possibility of military glory. His soft-spoken wife **Virgilia** harbors deep worries about her husband's expedition. Marcius lashes his troops to victory. He makes his way back to Rome, is given a hero's welcome, and is renamed Coriolanus to mark his accomplishment. The Senate nominates him as Consul; in order to win the office, the general reluctantly succombs to the custom requiring him to ask for the votes of Rome's citizens, whom he loathes. Two tribunes, **Brutus** and **Secinius**, talk the common people into withdrawing their support for Coriolanus. The office of Consul is denied to Coriolanus. He responds with venomous tirades against the common people, who in turn clamor for the general's death. A reconciliation is arranged, but when granted the opportunity to make amends with the populace, the proud Coriolanus is so enraged at the words of the tribunes that he erupts in fury yet again. As a result, he is banished from Rome. Disguised as a beggar, Coriolanus makes his way to Antium, where he encounters his rival Tullus Aufidius. The two make common cause against Rome, but Coriolanus's old rival knows that the alliance is not for the long term. **Cominius**, a fellow general of Coriolanus, begs in vain for the former Roman hero to spare the city. **Menenius Agrippa**, too, pleads that the attack be stayed, but to no avail. Finally, Coriolanus's mother, accompanied by his wife Virgilia and his son, succeed in their entreaty. Coriolanus's troops withdraw. At Corioli, Aufidius betrays his fellow general and accuses him of treachery against the cause of the Volsces. Coriolanus, confronted once again by an unruly mob, responds with his customary lack of verbal restraint. The result is chaos. Paid murderers stab Coriolanus to death. Aufidius suddenly repents his part in the great general's death, and swears to secure his "noble memory."

MINE! IT'S ALL MINE.

Keep an ear out for ongoing references to . . . The body and its various parts, illness, nobility, honor.

WHAT'S IT ALL ABOUT?

On one side, the intolerant and haughty general who nevertheless "hath deserved worthily of his country"; on the other, the fickle, dangerous mob. Shakespeare's mobs have a way of coming across as unruly, potentially destructive gatherings, and these mobs are no exception, but it would be a mistake to view this fact as the last word on Caius Martius Coriolanus and the class conflicts he incites. As usual, Shakespeare is presenting events with a vivid eye for detail and motivation, and adding resonance to the drama by refusing to take sides on certain key issues. In the end, *Coriolanus* is a play about the high cost of adamantly isolating oneself from the society in which one lives. The general's greatness of spirit is undeniable — but his belief in his own brutal power and self-sufficiency, long fostered by his mother, brings about catastrophe.

THE CRITICS' CORNER

"Anyone who studies it may save himself the trouble of reading Burke's *Reflections*, or Paine's *Rights of Man*, or the debates in both Houses of Parliament since the French Revolution or our own." (William Hazlitt)

"The subject of the whole play is not the exile's revolt, the rebel's repentance, or the traitor's reward, but above all it is the son's tragedy." (Algernon Charles Swinburne)

They say poor suitors have strong breaths; they shall know we have strong arms, too. (I, i)

I had rather had eleven die nobly for their country than one voluptiously surfeit out of action. (I, iii)

You are too absolute. (III, ii)

WHAT'S THE MATTER, YOU DISSENTIOUS ROGUES THAT, RUBBING THE POOR ITCH OF YOUR OPINION, MAKE YOURSELF SCABS? (I, i)

O my mother, mother! O!
You have won a happy victory for Rome;
But for your son — believe it, O believe it! —
Most dangerously you have with him prevailed,
If not most mortal to him. (V, iii)

I saw him run after a gilded butterfly; and when he caught it, he let it go again; and after it again; and over and over he comes, and up again; catched it again; or whether his fall engaged him, or how 'twas, he did so set his teeth, and tear it. (I, iii)

Did you perceive
He did solicit you in free contempt
When he did need your loves; and do you think
That his contempt shall not be bruising to youWhen he hath power to crush? (II, iii)

There was a time when all the body's members Rebell'd against the belly . . . (I,i)

. . . our virtues
Lie in the interpretation of the time (IV, vii)

171

Some cool things about Coriolanus

5: Coriolanus's complex relationships with his mother and with his rival Tullus Aufidius have given rise to plenty of psychosexual speculation.

4: Less is more department: Virgilia, like Cordelia in *King Lear* and Hero in *Much Ado About Nothing*, emerges as a distinctive presence despite comparatively little in the way of spoken lines.

3: A famous story about the play has it that a French production managed to incite both Fascists and Communists to riot, leading each group to believe that the play was intended as a political broadside against its cause.

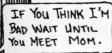

IF YOU THINK I'M BAD WAIT UNTIL YOU MEET MOM.

2: Aufidius's taunting reference to Coriolanus as a "boy of tears" initiates the final tirade from the Roman general.

1: After slaying Coriolanus, Aufidius "stands on him" (act V, scene vi), giving the lie to Volumnia's earlier prediction that Coriolanus would "tread on [Aufidius'] neck." (act I, scene iii)

Timon of Athens

Where lies the scene?
Ancient Athens

What happens?

A remarkably generous Athenian nobleman, **Timon**, is warned by the unpopular **Apemantus** that his smooth-talking friends are taking advantage of him. Timon's steward **Flavius** also tries to alert Timon to the consequences of his unlimited extravagance. Timon will hear none of it. We learn that Timon is very deeply in debt, and that his creditors are concerned about his ability to repay. He asks several of his "friends" for modest loans — and is turned down by each of them. His associates' true, exploitative nature dawns on Timon. He announces that he will be hosting a banquet. The friends who had denied him help all show up, and present less than convincing excuses for dodging or rejecting his messengers. The "banquet" consists only of warm water, which the guests find splashed in their faces. Timon curses his guests as opportunistic flatterers and orders them out of his house. In the Athenian Senate, the honored military man **Alcibiades** is banished by ungrateful Senators because he pleaded for the life of a worthy young soldier. Afterwards, he decides to assemble an army and march on Athens. Timon, embittered against all mankind, resolves to live apart from it. In a cave, he claws for roots to eat — and happens upon some buried treasure. When he encounters Alcibiades and learns that the soldier is intending to attack Athens, Timon passes along some of his treasure . . . but combines the gifts with the venomous bitterness that has become his only means of expression. Other visitors to the cave include the cynical Apemantus, some thieves who are surprised to hear their "victim" praise their line of work, and Timon's steward Flavius. Flavius's old master passes along a large chunk of the treasure — but on the condition that Flavius never return, and never undertake a charitable deed. A poet and a painter make their way to Timon's cave in search of his treasure. He reproaches them bitterly. The Senate seeks his help in repelling Alcibiades' attack. He offers them his fig tree and suggests that they hang themselves on it. Alcibiades reaches an accord with the leaders of Athens, and the innocent of the city are spared. Timon dies in his cave.

IF CHRIST HAD ALREADY BEEN BORN WE COULD CALL THIS CHRISTMAS — EXCEPT THIS IS EVERYDAY WITH ME!

Keep an ear open to ongoing references to . . . Flattery, flatterers, gold, extremity, dogs.

Wʜᴀᴛ's ɪᴛ ᴀʟʟ ᴀʙᴏᴜᴛ?

This difficult and extremely bitter play may well be a half-finished piece of work that Shakespeare abandoned after developing a preliminary draft. Whether the playwright considered it complete or not, a number of inconsistencies, gaps, and structural lapses make the play quite difficult to stage, and the general tone of loathing for all mankind makes it even more difficult to watch. *Timon* is not one of the Bard's most popular works. *Timon* doesn't grow or change for the better. As a result of experiences in the first half of the play, he comes to hate mankind; in the second half he never wavers from that hate, but instead simply restates it in a variety of ways. Although the early scenes can be fascinating if staged intelligently — the revelation that Timon's generosity is based on borrowed funds can be quite effective theatrically — the play's second section proves tough going for most spectators. The hero shouts insults at everyone and everything. There are not many plays in which Shakespeare requires so much indulgence from his audience as *Timon of Athens*. Although the play has its admirers (obviously, I'm not one of them), it is seldom produced. If Timon does represent an experiment that Shakespeare abandoned, he may have done so after staring long and hard at the stubborn fact that theatergoers are themselves members of the human race against which Timon rails so unceasingly.

> I THOUGHT IT WAS ALWAYS BETTER TO GIVE THAN RECEIVE— EVEN IF IT IS SOMEONE ELSE'S MONEY.

BE ABHORR'D
ALL FEASTS, SOCIETIES, AND THRONGS OF MEN!
HIS SEMBLANCE, YEA, HIMSELF TIMON DISDAINS:
DESTRUCTION FANG MANKIND!
(IV, iii)

I am not of that feather, to shake off
My friend when he most needs me. (I, i)

No villainous bounty yet hath pass'd my heart;
Unwisely, not ignobly, have I given. (II, ii)

Nothing emboldens sin so much as mercy. (III, v)

Uncover, dogs, and lap! (III, vi)

The middle of humanity thou never knewest, but the extremity of both ends. (IV, iii)

Graves only be men's works, and death their gain! (V, i)

Come not to me again, but say to Athens
Timon hath made his everlasting mansion
Upon the beached verge of the salt flood;
Who once a day with his embossed froth
The turbulent surge shall cover; thither come,
And let my gravestone be your oracle. (V, i)

THE CRITICS' CORNER

"(I)t is a dictionary of eloquent imprecations." (August Schlegel)

"(In *Timon of Athens*), Shakespeare stresses especially two properties of Money: (1) It is the visible divinity — the transformation of all human and natural properties into their contraries . . . (2) It is the common whore, the common pimp of peoples and nations." (Karl Marx)

"If Aristotle was right when he called plot the soul of tragedy, *Timon of Athens* has no soul." (Mark Van Doren)

Some cool things about Timon of Athens

5: Many passages in the second half of the play appear to capture Shakespeare in an "improvisational" mode. See, for instance, the portions of act IV, scene iii in which Timon and Apemantus exchange insults for long stretches. Around the same time, approaching characters are announced long before they materialize, presumably because the author thought of something else with which to fill up some stage time.

4: While *Timon* may not make for the best acting material, it offers an interesting (and rare) glimpse at what might be called a Beat vein in Shakespeare's writing. Perhaps his improvisational approach was a standard method of brainstorming in other plays he later edited heavily.

3: Shakespeare's often-expressed hatred of flattery and flatterers is given free rein in *Timon* as in no other play he ever wrote. At times, this loathing of people who offer false praise seems to take over the play.

2: Character check: Alcibiades, who has also been treated unjustly by the men of Athens, offers a sharp contrast to Timon. Instead of retreating into exile, Alcibiades takes action. He sets into motion a military campaign that concludes favorably, and without violence, thanks to a skill for compromise that the Athenian captain possesses but Timon lacks.

C.B., I'VE GOT A FABULOUS SCRIPT! HERE'S THE CONCEPT: SOCIETY SUCKS AND OUGHT TO BE DESTROYED!

1: There is no evidence that **Timon of Athens** was ever produced in Shakespeare's day.

WHERE LIES THE SCENE?

Antioch, Tyre, Tarsus, Pentapolis, Ephesus, Mytilene

WHAT HAPPENS?

In competing, under the threat of death, for the hand of the daughter of **Antiochus**, **Pericles**, the virtuous Prince of Tyre, realizes a terrible secret: the king and his daughter are engaged in an incestuous relationship. He leaves Antioch and returns to Tyre, but, fearful of the king's wrath, entrusts his kingdom to the noble **Helicanus** and sets out for Tarsus. No sooner has the prince left than an assassin arrives in Tyre with orders to murder him. Tarsus is undergoing a famine; when Pericles's ship arrives bearing food for the citizens, the governor welcomes him. But the prince soon learns that danger has followed him to Tarsus as well; he heads to sea again and is shipwrecked, losing his entire crew. Some fishermen return his lost armor to him, and he attends, as a knight, a celebration of the birthday of **Thaisa**, the daughter of the **King of Pentapolis**. He soon wins her favor and marries her, but does not reveal all the particulars of his past. When word reaches Pericles that King Antiochus has passed away, and that the nobles of his own land hope to crown Helicanus because they believe Pericles to have died, the prince explains his strange history and sets out for Tyre with his wife. A storm besets the unlucky Pericles; Thaisa is thought to have died during the journey while giving birth to their child, a girl. Pericles agrees to the sea burial of Thaisa, and, fearing that his infant daughter will not survive the journey to Tyre, makes for Tarsus, to leave the child in the care of his friend **Cleon**, the governor, and then return to Tyre. The unconscious thaisa, who has not in fact died, is shut up in a chest that washes up in Ephesus. A gifted physician restores her to full health. She enters upon a new life as a priestess of **Diana**. Years pass. Pericles's daughter, named **Marina**, is so beautiful and well esteemed that she arouses the jealousy of Cleon's wicked wife **Dionyza**, who believes her daughter **Philoten** to be suffering by comparison. Before the evil Dionyza can kill Marina, however, pirates carry away the innocent young woman and sell her into the service of a brothel-keeper in Myteline. There Marina is such a model of purity and grace that she dissuades Lysimachus, the governor of Mitylene, from succumbing to the sinful temptations of the house. She wins the respect of **Lysimachus** and virtuously talks her way out of the brothel. Pericles, believing the stories he has heard of his daughter's death, makes his way to Mitylene in sorrow — and is reunited with Marina. Following the urging of a dream, he takes his daughter to Ephesus, where the long-suffering family is reunited. Marina weds Lysimachus.

Keep an ear out for ongoing references to . . .
Fortune, journeys, separation, faithfulness, storms, jewels.

WHAT'S IT ALL ABOUT?

The distancing Chorus is presented by a character representing the poet John Gower, who wrote the source material. Gower's connective speeches lends a storybook feeling to the dreamlike series of comings and goings that mark the unlikely plot. (Scholars are divided as to Shakespeare's authorship of the Gower passages.) The play's unevenness in scale has haunted contemporary theatrical producers; unevenness of style is another problem. Most scholars feel that the first two acts reflect work primarily by an unknown author. Then there is the problem of the text: it seems to have been reconstructed from memory by actors. Beyond such difficulties, there is a play that has its moments, the brothel scenes and the father-daughter reunion in particular. Pericles is the first of the reconciliation-oriented "romances" that mark Shakespeare's great final phase as a dramatic writer. In this play, he creates a chaotic world where innocence somehow survives, where storms finally result not in destruction but in rebirth, and where a father and his daughter attain a measure of triumph over a hostile and turbulent world. The play serves as a kind of bridge between **King Lear** and **The Tempest**, and illustrates how important themes of redemption, rebirth, and harmony became to Shakespeare in his late period.

THE CRITICS' CORNER

"(I)n the final plays, that which is, the reality, does not break hearts; on the contrary, it is a cause for thanksgiving . . . . Rebirth through spring, through woman, acceptance of things as they are, but with a glory round them — that is what we find in all the plays from *Pericles* on." (Theodore Spencer)

"*Pericles* — the last three acts — is the swiftest and most lyrically conceived handling of the romance matter." (John F. Danby) ·

"We are talking about a hidden play, a play concealed from us by a text full of confusion and with a clumsiness and poverty of language unrivalled in the Shakespeare canon." (Philip Edwards)

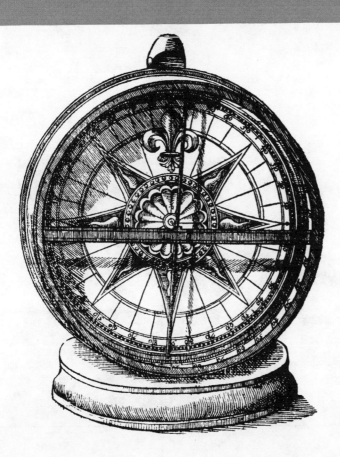

LINES TO LISTEN FOR

Third fisherman: Master, I marvel how the fishes live in the sea.
First fisherman: Why, as men do aland; the great ones eat up the little ones. (II, i)

> **A** terrible childbed hast thou had, my dear;
> No light, no fire; the unfriendly elements
> Forgot thee utterly; nor have I time
> To give the hallow'd to thy grave, but straight
> Must cast thee, scarcely coffin'd, in the ooze . . . (III, i)

Such a maidenhead were no cheap thing, if men were as they have been. (IV, ii)

Did you not name a
tempest,
A birth, and death? . . .
(V, iii)

He bears
A tempest, which his mortal
vessel tears,
And yet he rides
it out. (IV, iv)

DADDY.

5: Despite its general inaccessability to modern theater audiences, the play seems to have been a notable popular success in the seventeenth century.

4: *Pericles* was not among the plays included in the First Folio of 1623.

3: Beginning with this play, Shakespeare starts to focus intensely on issues of family separation and reunion. The same theme will reappear in *The Winter's Tale*, *Cymbeline*, and *The Tempest*.

> WE MUST GET FAMILIES TOGETHER AGAIN!

2: The importance of virtuous, resilient patience in the face of trial and adversity, which many critics see as the central message of the play, also appears at key moments of such plays as *King Lear*. ("Ripeness is all," Edgar counsels Gloucester in *Lear*.)

1: Percles's reunion with Marina strongly recalls that of King Lear with Cordelia.

CYMBELINE

WHERE LIES THE SCENE?
Britain and Rome

WHAT HAPPENS?

Imogen, only daughter of **King Cymbeline**, has married the worthy but lowly **Posthumus** rather than **Cloten**, son of the Queen by another marriage. Infuriated, Cymbeline banishes Posthumus, who gives his wife Imogen a striking bracelet before they part, and recieves in turn a diamond ring that he promises to wear faithfully. When he reaches Rome, he meets the villainous **Iachimo**, who induces him to wager the ring on his wife's fidelity. Iachimo goes to Britain and arranges a meeting with Imogen, after which he realizes that she cannot be seduced. Iachimo hides in a chest that Imogen has agreed to keep an eye on for him. In her room, he emerges after she falls asleep and takes the bracelet Posthumus gave to her. Back in Italy, he shows off the bracelet and manages to fool Posthumus into believing that his wife has betrayed him. The arrogant Cloten attempts, with no success, to win over Imogen; the idea of betraying her husband is unthinkable to the virtuous daughter of the king. Lucius, ambassador from Rome, demands tribute from Cymbeline; under the influence of Cloten and his mother, the king challenges the Roman representative, and war soon follows. In Italy, Posthumus orders his servant **Pisanio** to put Imogen to death. Yet Pisanio is convinced that Imogen is innocent; he helps her make her way from the court disguised as a page. Imogen ends up in the hills of Wales, where she finds an exiled nobleman named **Belarius**, who, twenty years earlier, abducted the two infant sons of Cymbeline, now named **Guiderus** and **Arviragus**. Their identity is kept a secret to all. Imogen's disappearance from court causes a stir; Pisanio attempts to mislead Cloten as to her whereabouts. As it happens, however, Cloten makes his way to Belarius's dwelling disguised as Posthumus; in a fight with one of the sons, he is beheaded. Imogen takes a potion (originally intended for Pisanio) that she believes to be a restorative, and that the scheming queen had intended to be poison. In fact, thanks to the earlier influence of the virtuous physician Cornelius, it only has a stupefying effect. The brothers find her and believe her to be dead. They take the seemingly lifeless body into the woods, place it on the ground next to the headless trunk of Cloten, and strew the area with flowers.

I KNOW YOU'RE POSTHUMOUS, BUT ARE YOU POSTHUMUS?

Imogen awakens, only to see the body of a beheaded man dressed in her husband's clothing — and swoons. Lucius enters as she regains herself and takes the "page" on as his attendant. Iachimo, having raised a military force, is preparing to invade Britain from Gaul. The evil queen loses her sanity as a result of her son's having vanished. Guiderus and Arviragus, eager to defend their homeland, itch for battle. Posthumus, who has come back to Britain, disguises himself as a lowly peasant and, full or remorse, hopes to die in battle against the attackers from Gaul. In league with Belarius, Guiderus, and Arviragus, he fights heroically, and does not perish. He falsely claims to be a Roman in the hope of being executed, and is imprisoned. In captivity, he has a striking prophetic vision involving Jupiter. The queen dies, but not before confessing her evil deeds. Lucius, his page (in reality, Imogen), and Iachimo are all captured and brought before the

king; Posthumus, too, is made to appear before Cymbeline. In Cymbeline's presence the disguised Imogen engineers a confession from Iachimo. Posthumus reveals his true identity; Imogen reveals hers; Guiderus and Arviragus are discovered to be the long-lost sons of the king.. A pardon is extended to Belarius and to the Roman ambassador, and peace is secured with Rome.

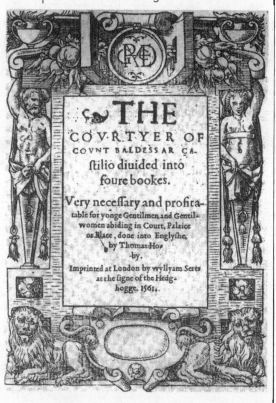

SEE, DADDY, HE'S A REAL SLUGGER ONCE YOU GET TO KNOW HIM.

What Happens?

Cymbeline, which boasts what may well be Shakespeare's most contrived and intricate plot is a fairy tale and Imogen, the utterly faithful and well-spoken woman at the center of it, is meant to build, more or less from scratch, a husband who does not really deserve her.

In addition to its incredibly complicated story, the play features an unusually high number of linguistic backflips, a strange and unprepared-for appearance by the god Jupiter, and a "we're-outta-here-folks" final scene packed with revelation after revelation. Critics have assailed these extreme elements, but in a way extremity may be the point. In a fairy-tale world, the powers that be play strange games with mortals, as they do in *A Midsummer Night's Dream*. Here, the struggles are greater and the possibilities are more dangerous. But with a patient enough heroine, joyous reunion after the hazards is still possible.

The Critics' Corner

"This play has many just sentiments, some natural dialogues, and some pleasing scenes, but they are obtained at the expense of much incongruity." (Samuel Johnson)

"Every reader of this play loves this radiant and spirited girl; what more natural than to dislike the husband who makes her suffer?" (William Witherle Lawrence)

LINES TO LISTEN FOR

She punish'd for her truth, and undergoes,
More goddess-like than wife-like, such assaults
As would take in some virtue. (III, ii)

REVENG'D?
HOW SHOULD I BE REVENG'D. IF THIS BE TRUE
(AS I HAVE SUCH A HEART THAT BOTH MINE EARS
MUST NOT IN HASTE ABUSE), IF IT BE TRUE,
HOW SHOULD I BE REVENG'D?
(I, vi)

I see a man's life is a tedious one. (III, vi)

Golden
lads and girls all must,
As chimney-sweepers, come to
dust. (IV, ii)

Fortune brings in some boats that are not steer'd. (IV, iii)

Hang there like fruit, my soul, Till the tree die! (V, v)

Keep an ear out for ongoing references to . . .
Nature, trees, birds, purchase and sale, value.

5: The play is one of the later reconciliation-oriented dramas, or romances; it emphasizes the redemptive power of a young woman on a complex and difficult world.

4: Despite the intricacy and occasional difficulty of the play as a whole, Imogen has won her share of admiration as one of Shakespeare's pluckiest heroines.

3: The exquisite dirge that appears in Act Four ("Fear no more the heat of the sun . . .") is one of the play's most moving scenes. The song's tone seems to predict some of the most moving passages in the later play *The Tempest*.

2: While mourning the supposed death of his wife in Act V, scene v, Posthumus — who has previously contrived to have Imogen murdered — strikes her while she is disguised as a page!

1: George Bernard Shaw rewrote the difficult final act of the play, streamlining it and observing that "(p)lot has always been the curse of serious drama."

WHERE LIES THE SCENE?

Sicilia and Bohemia

WHAT HAPPENS?

King **Leontes** of Sicilia suspects his wife **Hermione** of having had an affair with **Polixenes**, the King of Bohemia. Leontes attempts to put Polixenes to death by poison, but the Bohemian king escapes. Hermione is sent to prison, where she delivers a daughter. **Paulina**, a Sicilian noblewoman, brings the infant girl to Leontes, hoping to sway him toward tenderness, but the king has closed his heart. He orders Paulina's husband, **Antigonus**, to abandon the child by the shore. An oracle instructs the king of Hermione's innocence; Leontes still refuses to set her at liberty. **Mamillus**, the kings's son, dies of sadness at the mistreatment of Hermione, who swoons at the news. Later, Paulina tells the king Hermione has died. Leontes repents. The infant (**Perdita**) is abandoned; Antigonus is slain by a bear. A shepherd finds the girl and raises her. Years pass. The child grows into lovely young country woman and falls in love with **Florizel**, son of **Polixenes**. A ballad peddler, **Autolycus**, engages in humorous rogueries. Florizel and Polixenes decide to flee Bohemia with the shepherd in order to escape Polixenes' wrath; the Bohemian king disapproves of their union because of Perdita's (supposed) low birth. The lovers arrive in Sicilia, where Perdita's true identity is revealed to Leontes. Polixenes is reconciled with Leontes; when the Bohemian king discovers Perdita's true identity he agrees to her marriage with Florizel. Leontes rejoices at having found his daughter — and mourns again the loss of his wife. Paulina proposes to show the King a statue that is the exact likeness of Hermione. When he sees it, his agony only increases, until the statue seems to come to life. It is in fact Hermione, alive and well, whose death had been reported to spare her from Leontes's fury.

191

What's it all about?

A chorus representing Time helps to span the sixteen-year interval between acts III and IV. This is a structural example of seemingly insurmountable division, the same type of division that comes between Leontes and Hermione, Leontes and Perdita, and Leontes and Polixenes. Although the play supplies happy endings on all fronts (in keeping with a story meant for long winter's nights), the somber tone of the piece as a whole suggests that Shakespeare is dealing with hard, not always comforting truths related to obsession and redemption from it. Nature has a way of overcoming obstacles. The "revival" of Hermione is enacted — quite effectively — onstage, while the reunion of Perdita and Leontes is not. Perhaps Shakespeare felt he had already written, in *King Lear* and *Pericles*, enough in the way of father-daughter reunions; perhaps the plot turned out to be a little too crowded for its own good; perhaps Shakespeare simply decided there was more to be gained by emphasizing the possibility of a springlike renewal of an older character whose "statue" supposedly presents her wrinkles and all, "as she liv'd now."

The critics' corner

"[O]ver and around this drama particularly a religious atmosphere hovers. There is in it a certain otherworldliness which we shall hardly find elsewhere in Shakespeare to the same extent . . . it touches questions which are usually considered theological." (Denton J. Snider)

"It is a story of the divisions created in love and friendship by the passage of Time and the action of 'blood,' and of the healing of these divisions. The play turns upon an organic relationship between breakdown and reconstruction . . . " (D.A. Traversi)

Lines to listen for:

We were, fair queen,
Two lads that thought there was no more behind [to come]
But such a day tomorrow as today
And to be boy eternal. (I, ii)

Hermione is chaste, Polixenes blameless, Camillo a true subject, Leontes a jealous tyrant, his innocent babe truly begotten, and the king shall live without an heir, if that which is lost be not found. (III, ii)

O, THAT IS ENTERTAINMENT MY BOSOM LIKE NOT, NOR MY BROWS! (I, ii)

What's gone and what's past help
Should be past grief. (III, ii)

These your unusual weeds to each part of you
Does give a life . . . (IV, iv)

I think affliction may subdue the cheek,
But not take in the mind. (IV, iv)

A merry heart goes all the day;
Your sad tires in a mile-a (IV, iii)

Autolycus: here's another ballad, of a fish that appear'd upon the coast on We'n'sday the fourscore of April, forty thousand fadom above water, and sung this ballad against the hard hearts of maids . . . .
Dorcas: Is it true, too, think you?
Auolycus: Five justices' hands to it, and witnesses more than my pack will hold. (IV, iv)

. . . **A**n old tale still, which will have matter to rehearse, though credit [belief] be asleep and not an ear open. (V, ii)

> **I**t is requir'd
> You do awake your faith. (V, iii)

Comes it not something near? (V, iii)

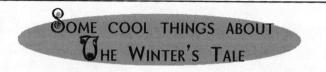

Some cool things about The Winter's Tale

5: Hermione's return to life represents a triumph over death reminiscent of those that appear in the earlier comedies. In this play, however, it is no youthful lover who "comes back to life," but a wronged, decidedly mature wife and mother.

4: Ben Jonson ridiculed Shakespeare's decision to place a shipwreck in landlocked Bohemia.

3: The play is based on part of Robert Greene's 1588 novel *Pandosto*. In the original, the wronged queen dies.

2: Scholars are divided on the question of how the bear was represented onstage.

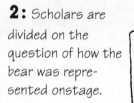

1: Examination of the roles of art and nature, and of human faith as it relates to both, occupies an important place in the play.

WHERE LIES THE SCENE?
A strange island

WHAT HAPPENS?

A terrible storm besieges a ship that carries **King Alonso** of Naples and members of his party. Thanks to the magical intervention of **Prospero**, who initiated the storm, the ship wrecks on a strange island no loss of life, although the passengers are separated. We learn that Prospero, the Duke of Milan, years before, was wrongly deprived of his throne by **Antonio**, his brother, acting in league with the king. Prospero was abandoned at sea with his young daughter **Miranda**; eventually, the two came ashore upon the magic island, which had previously served as a banishing-place for the witch **Sycorax**. For twelve years Prospero and Miranda have lived here; Prospero's proficiency in magic allowed him to set free spirits, including **Ariel**, his servant, and the enslaved monster **Caliban**, Sycorax's son — who fell into disfavor with Prospero when he attempted to rape Miranda. The virtuous **Gonzalo** tries to comfort the king, who believes his son **Ferdinand** has perished in the shipwreck. The two fall asleep when Ariel casts a spell on them. Antonio and Sebastian, Alonso's brother, plot to kill the king. Ariel awakens the sleeping pair.

Caliban encounters the fool **Trinculo** and the drunken butler Stephano. They give him wine, and he vows to worship them as gods. Ferdinand, set to work by Prospero, falls in love with Miranda. Caliban, Trinculo, and Stephano drunkenly discuss a plot to kill Prospero, steal his books, and take over the island. A banquet appears and disappears; Ariel, in the form of a Harpy, warns the hungry king and his companions that Ferdinand's loss is retribution for past sins. Alonso leaves, hoping to find his son's body and die where it lies. Prospero agrees to the engagement of Ferdinand to his daughter, and tells Ariel to provide celebratory entertainment. The subsequent masque is interrupted when Prospero remembers the plot against his life by Caliban and his companions. He tricks them and sets spirits disguised as dogs after them. Prospero sends Ariel to collect the shaken king, Antonio, Sebastian, and Gonzalo. He promises to show mercy to his past tormentors, and, once his business is done, to abandon magic forever. His enemies reconcile themselves to Prospero and restore his dukedom. Ferdinand is reunited with his son. We learn that the ship has been restored to working order. Prospero orders Ariel to supply favorable weather for the trip back to Milan — and then sets the spirit free.

ANIMAL I CALLED You— THAT 'SEXY' YOU ADDED.

Keep an ear out for ongoing references to:

Storms, thunder, sound, music, impermanence, the limits of human power and authority.

You I Call O'RIEL!

WHAT'S IT ALL ABOUT?

In this powerful, dreamlike play, Shakespeare seems to channel all that has worked magic in his earlier dramas into a single magical piece of theater. Many consider *The Tempest* his greatest achievement. Like Henry V, another man who confronts representatives of a corrupt, complicated human society, Prospero is completely successful in his efforts to transcend and remake that society. On the surface, the two men couldn't be more different: Henry grows into a pragmatic, vigorous politician-warrior, and Prospero has become a wise and tested sorcerer. Yet each man knows the limits of human nature and authority (including his own), and each has mental resolve strong enough to resolve past wrongs and bring about a new kind of society, seemingly by force of will. Prospero is the last and greatest of Shakespeare's protagonists to serve as an onstage "dramatist," controlling and directing the events around him. He seems to be not only the hero of this play, but somehow of all the previous plays as well. In *The Tempest*, the foiled plots and conspiracies of evil people, the final triumph of both innocence and age, the banishment of animal selfishness — all these seem parts of a far larger story than the play we're watching. They seem relevant to the great, impermanent human drama we all create day by day.

"The great and striking peculiarity of the action of (The Tempest) is that it lies wholly in the Ideal World." (Denton J. Snider)

"(The Masque scene in IV, i) show(s) a spirit untrammelled by ties in the present, undistracted by hopes for the future . . it is the mood of one who, contemplating all time and all existence, sees them as some sublime dramatic poem, moving inevitably and harmoniously towards 'a full and natural close, like music.' " (J. Dover Wilson)

LINES TO LISTEN FOR

... the dark backward and abysm of time. (I, ii)

WE ARE SUCH STUFF AS DREAMS ARE MADE ON, AND OUR LITTLE LIFE IS ROUNDED WITH A SLEEP.
(IV, i)

You are a councillor; if you can command these elements to silence, and work the peace of the present, we will not hand a rope more. Use your authority. If you cannot, give thanks you have liv'd so long, and make yourself ready in your cabin for the mischance of the hour . . . (I, i)

What is past is prologue. (II, i)

O brave new world,
That has such people in't! (V, i)

Though with their high wrongs I am struck to th' quick,
Yet with my nobler reason 'gainst my fury
Do I take part. The rarer action is
In virtue than in vengeance. They being penitent,
The sole drift of my purpose doth extend
Not a frown further. Go, release them, Ariel. (V, i)

 ## SOME COOL THINGS ABOUT THE TEMPEST

5: Many of the earlier comedies point their characters toward a special, transforming place (such as the forest of Arden in *As You Like It*) that contrast sharply with the characters' everyday experience. They leave the "real" world, visit the unusual place, and then return to help fashion a new and better society. In *The Tempest*, the entire play takes place in this renewing environment.

4: Prospero's famous speech that begins "Our revels now are ended" (IV, i) is preceded by a strange outburst from the sorcerer, who remembers the plot against his life — and perhaps evil itself — before delivering his discourse on the transient nature of all human experience.

3: *The Tempest* is the only one of Shakespeare's plays set in the New World.

2: The film *Prospero's Books* — out on video — provides a hallucinatory, visually dense adaptation of the play, and boasts an unforgettable performance from Sir John Gielgud as Prospero.

1: Nothing lasts in this life of ours. But that's okay.

BILL, HAVE YOU FORGOTTEN ME?

OF COURSE NOT, ROBBY. YOUR TURN AS 'ARIEL' IN "FORBIDDEN PLANET" WAS SIMPLY RADIOACTIVE!

Speech bubble: DON'T TOUCH THAT DIAL! THERE'S MORE! IN ADDITION TO THE PLAYS, YOU ALSO GET...

The Poems

Venus And Adonus (early 1590s)

An entertaining, erotic long poem relating the goddess Venus's pursuit of the physically alluring, but distinctly mortal, Adonis. Venus wants to do the deed with the strapping young man; he'd prefer to hunt. The following day, Adonis is killed by a wild boar, after which Venus laments his passing.

Seeds spring from seeds, and beauty breedeth beauty.
Thou wast begot; to get [beget] it is thy duty.
(Lines 167-168)

Poor queen of love, in thine own law forlorn,
To love a cheek that smiles at thee in scorn!
(Lines 251-252)

The path is smooth that leadeth on to danger.
(Line 788)

WHAT'S A GODDESS GOTTA DO TO GET A GUY? WEAR CAMOUFLAGE?

THE CRITICS' CORNER

"(The poem reveals) Shakespeare's loving familiarity with Ovid, whose effects he fuses . . ." (George Wyndham)

"If Venus and Adonis were wholly bookish, a piece of pure tapestry, all would be well. But for an orgy of the senses it is too unreal, for a decorative pseudo-classic picture it has too much homely realism." (Douglas Bush)

"Although she lacks Cleopatra's infinite variety, Venus is nonetheless the earliest intimation of Shakespeare's power to create his great, tragic, wanton queen."(Rufus Putney)

The Rape of Lucrece
(early 1590s)

An expanded, rhetorically intense poetic retelling of a story from Livy about the Roman Tarquin's violation of the virtuous, married Lucretia (Lucrece). After the dastardly deed is done, Shakespeare focuses on the victimized woman's horror and shame, and on her resulting suicide, which is presented as a noble and honorable response to her situation. The poem takes a high moral tone that contrasts with the more light-hearted Venus and Adonis.

Her breasts like ivory globes circled with blue,
A pair of maiden worlds unconquered,
Save of their lord no bearing yoke they knew,
And him by oath they truly honored.
These worlds in Tarquin new ambition bred,
Who like a foul usurper went about
From this fair throne to heave the owner out. (Lines
407-413)

THE CRITICS' CORNER

"(U)ninspired and pitilessly prolix . . .
(it) could have no unstudious readers in
our day and few warm admirers in (its) own . . ."
(John M. Robertson)

"Until the crime is committed, Tarquin is the focus of our
attention, and convinces us that he is a tragically complex
character. After the deed, Lucrece becomes the tragic heroine;
but we are never wholly convinced that she deserves the part .
. . she is forced to express herself in a way which dissipates
the real pathos of her situation." **(F.T. Prince)**

**"It mirrors faithfully the defective actions of noble persons
and the sad consequences which coherently ensue." (Roy W.
Battenhouse)**

The Sonnets

(dates of composition uncertain)

These are what people usually talk about when they talk about Shakespeare's non-dramatic poetry: 154 finely wrought poems, perhaps composed at various points in the 1590s. Some of them are hailed as among the finest poems in English.

The sonnets fall into two groups: All the poems, with the exception of number 126, which is twelve lines long, follow a fourteen-line pattern, with a distinct rhyme scheme: abab cdcd efef gg. Many of the poems in the group 1-126 seem to be addressed to a young man, a friend of the poet's; numbers 127-154, on the other hand, feature poems directed to a darkly featured woman, addressed as the poet's difficult lover. She has come to be known as the **"Dark Lady."**

Are the people referenced in these poems real, or simply literary devices? Many have tried to turn the sonnets into a kind of autobiography of Shakespeare. This is interesting enough, and some of the sonnets certainly do seem likely to be rooted in personal experience, but few if any direct conclusions about the facts of Shakespeare's life can be drawn from the poems.

AWRIGHT NOW, SIR, IF YOU WOULD PLEASE IDENTIFY THE 'DARK LADY'.

Whether or not they reflect real-life personal entanglements, these varied poems are dense and powerful, demanding
and breathtaking. Unlike the plays, they are designed to be
read, rather than enacted; unlike the longer narrative poems,
they tend to bring readers back again and again. No short
summary can do them justice. Start by reading the full ver-
sions of the sonnets excerpted below; you'll probably find yourself hooked before too long.

LIKE AS THE WAVES TOWARD THE PEBBLED SHORE,
SO DO OUR MINUTES HASTEN TO THEIR END.
(SONNET 60)

Summer's lease hath all too short a date. **(Sonnet 18)**

For thy sweet love remember'd such wealth brings
That then I scorn to change my state with kings. **(Sonnet 29)**

Nor marble nor the gilded monuments
Of princes shall outlive this pow'rful rhyme,
But you shall shine more bright in these contents
Than unswept stone, besmear'd with sluttish time. **(Sonnet 55)**

To me, fair friend, you never can be old,
For as you were when first your eye I ey'd
Such seems your beauty still. **(Sonnet 104)**

FOR I HAVE SWORN
   THEE FAIR,
   AND THOUGHT THEE BRIGHT,
WHO ART AS BLACK AS HELL,
AS DARK AS NIGHT.
      (SONNET 147)

Let me not to the marriage of true minds
Admit impediments; love is not love
Which alters when it alteration finds
Or bends with the remover to remove. **(Sonnet 116)**

When my love swears that she is made of truth,
I do believe her, though I know she lies,
That she might think me some untutor'd youth,
Unlearned in the world's false subtleties. **(Sonnet 138)**

THE CRITICS' CORNER

"The subject of them seems to be somewhat equivocal; but many of them are highly beautiful in themselves, and interesting as they relate to the state of the personal feelings of the author." (William Hazlitt)

"In the best sonnets the wordplay is neither involuntary nor wilful; it is a skilfully handled means whereby Shakespeare makes explicit both his conflict of feelings and his resolutions of the conflict." (M. M. Mahood)

"Each poem needs to be dwelt on; each requires the kind of concentrated attention which would have been given when they were received singly or in small groups." (C.L. Barber)

The Phoenix And The Turtle

(early 1600s)

An allegorical poem that concerns itself with idealized, mystical love; the phoenix represents immortality, and the turtle (we would say "turtledove") represents faithfulness. The pair of birds have joined in eternal love by burning themselves alive, the idea being that a completely spiritual love relationship requires not sexual union, but a common willingness to cast off the world through death. Although this approach seems foolish by worldly standards, it offers sublime union.

Two distincts, division none:
Number there in love was slain. (Lines 27-28)

Reason in itself confounded,
Saw division grow together. (Lines 41-42)

"This poem, if published for the first time and without a known author's name, would find no general reception. Only the poets would save it." (Ralph Waldo Emerson)

"We feel . . . as though we had reached the gardon of Adonis and seen where Imogens and Cordelias are made." (C.S. Lewis)

"Into The Phoenix and the Turtle, fantastic as it is, Shakespeare has compressed all his feeling for pure passion and loyalty in human love." (F.T. Prince)

OTHER POEMS

The Passionate Pilgrim (a collection of poems by a number of authors) and *A Lover's Complaint* (a relatively short poetic monologue by a betrayed young woman) are minor pieces that have incited vigorous, and dry, scholarly debate about Shakespeare's contributions to them.

TH-TH-THAT'S ALL FOLKS!

Bibliography/Further Reading

📖 **Alexander, Peter,** <u>Shakespeare's Life and Art</u>. New York University Press, New York, 1939.

📖 **Boyce, Charles,** <u>Shakespeare A to Z</u>. Facts on File, New York, 1990.

📖 **Bradbook, M.C.,** <u>Fifty Years of the Criticism of Shakespeare's Style: A Retrospect</u>. Shakespeare Survey, Volume 7, New York, 1954.

📖 **Eastman, A.M. and G.B. Harrison, editors,** <u>Shakespeare's Critics, University of Michigan Press</u>, Ann Arbor, 1964.

📖 **Evans, G. Blakemore, textual editor,** <u>The Riverside Shakespeare</u>, Houghton Mifflin, Boston, 1974.

📖 **Fox, Levi,** <u>The Shakespeare Handbook</u>. G.K. Hall & Company, Boston, 1987.

📖 **Harris, Laurie Lanzen, and Mark W. Scott, editors,** <u>Shakespearean Criticism</u>, Gale Research Company, Detroit, Michigan, 1984.

📖 **Johnson, Samuel,** <u>Johnson on Shakespeare</u>. (Arthur Sherbo, editor.) Yale University Press, New Haven, 1968.

📖 **Knight, G. Wilson,** <u>The Wheel of Fire: Interpretations of Shakespearean Tragedy</u>. World Publishing/Meridian Books, Cleveland, 1957.

📖 **Ridler, Ann, editor,** <u>Shakespeare Criticism</u>. Oxford University Press, New York, 1951.

📖 **Spurgeon, Caroline F.E.,** <u>Shakespeare's Imagery and What It Tells Us</u>, Beacon Press, Boston, 1958.

📖 **Stoll, E.E.,** <u>Art and Artifice in Shakespeare</u>. Cambridge University Press, Cambridge, 1934.

📖 **Tillyard , E.M.W.,** <u>The Elizabethan World Picture</u>. Macmillan, New York, 1943.

📖 **Van Doren, Mark,** <u>Shakespeare</u>. , Doubleday Anchor, Garden City, New York, 1955.

📖 **Zesmer,** <u>David M. Guide to Shakespeare</u>, Barnes & Noble Books, New York, 1976.

📖 _____., <u>The Harvard Concordance to Shakespeare</u>. Harvard University Press, Cambridge, Massachusetts, 1973.

VIDEOS (ETCETERA) WORTH A LOOK

Hamlet (1997) — An earnest, direct, and extremely satisfying full-text assault on the world's most-discussed play. How Branagh escaped an Oscar nomination remains a mystery.

Looking for Richard (1996) — Al Pacino's innovative semidocumentary take on Richard III

Henry V (1989) — Kenneth Branagh's masterpiece.

Ran (1984) — Kurasawa's retelling of King Lear.

King Lear (1984) — Laurence Olivier's last leading role and it's a doozy.

The Taming of the Shrew (1967) — Elizabeth Taylor, Richard Burton, Franco Zefferelli. Magical.

A Midsummer Night's Dream (1935) — The Warner Brothers machine tries its hand at love, moonlight, and illusions. It works!

And, if it's still playing in theaters:
Umabatha: The Zulu Macbeth —

❀ CAST OF CHARACTERS ❀

Two Gentlemen Of Verona
Laurel & Hardy

Henry VI
Woody Allen
Judy Garland (as Joan Of Ark)

Richard III
Dick Nixon

Comedy Of Errors
Buster Keaton
Sammy Davis Jr.

Titus Andronicus
Arnold Schwartzenegger

Taming Of The Shrew
Lucy & Desi

Love's Labor Lost
3 Stooges & Shemp

Romeo & Juliet
James Dean as both

Richard II
Elvis

A Midsummer Night's Dream
Pee Wee Herman as Puck
Anna Nicole Smith as Titania
Bert Lahr as Bottom
Charlton Heston as Theseus

King John
Prince Charles & Mum

Merchant Of Venus
Donald Trump
with a cameo by J.P. Morgan

Henry V
F.D.R.
W.C. Fields
J.F.K.
with William "Tecumsah" Sherman supporting

Much Ado About Nothing
The Honeymooners (all 4)

Henry IV
J.F.K.
Charles De Gaule

Julius Ceaser
Al Capone
Edward G. Robinson

Twelfth Night
Uncle Miltie
William Blake

As You Like It
Marlene Dietrich
Charlie Chaplin
Gorgeous George

Merry Wives Of Windsor
W.C. Fields

Hamlet
Samuel Beckett
Marilyn Monroe

Troilus & Cressida
Ava Gardner
Lenny Bruce

All's Well...
Lillian Gish
Valentino

Measure For Measure
Jimmy Swaggert

King Lear
Sigmund Freud
Groucho Marx

Othello
J. Edgar Hoover

Macbeth
Joseph Stalin
Leon Trotsky
Madonna

Anthony & Cleopatra
Jessie Norman
Clark Gable

Coriolanus
Picasso

Timon Of Athens
Mark Twain

Pericles
Jimmy Carter
Andy Warhol

Cymbeline
Teddy Roosevelt
Babe Ruth
Audry Hepburn

Winter's Tale
Salvador Dali

Tempest
Albert Einstein
Jack Nicholson
Quentin Crisp
Robby The Robot

Venus & Adonis
Sophia Loren

Sonnets-Dark Lady
Grace Jones
My Fiance, Bess
Paloma Picasso
Tina Turner
Shelley Duval

Pheonix & Turtle
Lewis Carroll's Griffen & Mock
Turtle

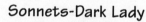

AUTHOR:

Brandon Toropov is a playwright, author, and confirmed Shakespeare fanatic who lives in Massachusetts. His plays include *Seven Affidavits on Authority,* produced in Boston and Providence, Rhode Island, in 2000; *An Undivided Heart,* workshopped at the National Playwrights Conference in 1994; and *The Job Search,* produced at the Manhattan Punch Line in 1987. As an actor, he has performed in productions or adaptations of *The Tempest, A Midsummer Night's Dream,* and *Macbeth.* He has authored over a dozen books on popular culture, business, and religion, including *Who Was Eleanor Rigby?, The Complete Idiot's Guide to Urban Legends,* and *The Complete Idiot's Guide to the Koran.*

ILLUSTRATOR:

Joe Lee is an illustrator, cartoonist, writer and clown. A graduate of Ringling Brothers, Barnum and Bailey's Clown College, he worked for many years as a circus clown. He is also the illustrator for many other For Beginners books including: *Dada and Surrealism For Beginners, Postmodernism For Beginners, Deconstruction For Beginners, The Olympics For Beginners* and *Existentialism For Beginners.* Joe lives with his wife, Mary Bess, three cats, and two dogs (Toby and Jack).